LEVEL BEST

1

DELIVERING
THE FRAMEWORK
FOR TEACHING
▌▌ENGLISH ▌▌

Michael Ross ▌▌ *Keith West*
Series Consultant: *Mike Hamlin*

Published in 2001 by:
Nelson Thornes Ltd
Delta Place
27 Bath Road
CHELTENHAM
GL53 7TH
United Kingdom

01 02 03 04 05 / 10 9 8 7 6 5 4 3 2 1

A catalogue record for this book is available from the British Library

ISBN 0-7487-6058-X

Illustrations by Jim Eldridge, Linda Jeffrey, Richard Johnson, Angela Lumley, Zhenya Matysiak, Mick Stubbs and Harry Venning
Edited by Melanie Gray
Designed by Holbrook Design Oxford Limited

Printed and bound in Spain by Graficas Estella

Acknowledgements

The authors and publishers wish to thank the following for permission to reproduce copyright material and photographs in this book:

Bloomsbury Publishing Plc for material from Caroline Alexander, *Mrs Chippy's Last Expedition: The Remarkable Journal of Shackleton's Polar-Bound Cat*, pp. 155–7, 148, 150;

David Calcutt for material from his adaption of *Homer's Odyssey*, Nelson (1999) pp.12–14, 17–9, 21–2, 25–6;

Cambridge University Press for material from Steve Fitzpatrick, 'The Cyclops' from *The Lost Ring and Other Plays* by Steve Fitzpatrick (1985) pp. 70–3, 75–7, 90–2;

Centre for Alternative Technology for material from CAT 'Discover' leaflet and CAT 'Something for Everyone' poster;

Express Newspapers Ltd for 'Messages by mobile ruin children's English', *The Express*, 2.9.00;

Faber and Faber Ltd for George Szirtes, 'The more you hold him' and 'I know a man – he lives in the wall' from *The Red All Over Riddle Book* by George Szirtes (1998); and an extract from Seamus Heaney, 'The Errand' from *The Spirit Level* by Seamus Heaney (1996);

John Foster for 'Riddle – My first is in fish but not in chip' included in *The Works*, ed. Paul Cookson, Macmillan (2000). Copyright © John Foster 2000;

David Higham Associates on behalf of the author for Penelope Lively, 'Next Term We'll Mash You' from *Pack of Cards* by Penelope Lively, Heinemann (1986);

IKEA for a quote from their 2001 IKEA Catalogue;

Independent Newspapers (UK) Ltd for Susannah Prain, 'Four pints is good for you. Water, that is', *The Independent*, 24.8.00;

Mike Jenkins, for 'Acrobats' plus explanatory text;

McCann-Erickson for press release, 'Du Spk Text?', 8.8.00;

Judith Nicholls for 'Riddle (I am word-cruncher...)'. Copyright © Judith Nicholls 1996;

Penguin Books Ltd for material from Michelle Magorian, *Goodnight Mister Tom*, Kestrel (1981) pp. 17, 19, 22, 74, 75–7, 182, 192. Copyright © Michelle Magorian 1981;

Peters Fraser and Dunlop Group Ltd on behalf of the Estate of David Wright for material from *The Canterbury Tales*, translated by David Wright. Copyright © David Wright 1964;

Seren for Sheenagh Pugh, 'Tutorial' from *Stonelight*, Seren Books (1999);

Times Newspapers Ltd for David Charter, 'E-mail sends coded warning to English teachers', *The Times*, 2.9.00. Copyright © Times Newspapers Ltd 2000; and 'Sir E Shackleton's Story', *The Times*, 2nd June 1916. Copyright © Times Newspapers Ltd 1916;

A P Watt Ltd on behalf of the author for an extract from Philip Pullman, *Northern Lights*, Scholastic (1995) pp. 226–7;

The Bridgeman Art Library p. 116; The British Library p. 28; Cotswold Spring Natural Mineral Water pp. 8, 10; Department of Transport, Environment and the Regions for advertisement pp. 6, 7; Parliamentary Education Unit p. 70; Photofusion p. 69; Scott Polar Research Institute pp. 18, 20.

Every effort has been made to contact the copyright holders. The publishers apologise to anyone whose rights have been inadvertently overlooked, and will be happy to rectify any errors or omissions.

Contents

Introduction

You're going to be using a book that is designed to help you make real progress – do your level best – in English. You'll get the most out of the book if you know something about why it is written in the way it is.

- At the beginning of each unit there is a statement telling you about the purpose of the unit ('Your focus'). Here you also find out what skills you will be developing over the unit ('Your target'). It obviously helps you to achieve an aim if you know clearly what the aim is. You will also be able to see at a glance how the unit is structured in terms of facilities ('Your move').

- In many of the activities you will first of all have a chance to discuss questions in small groups. This means you can try out ideas which you might not want to say straightaway to everyone. Your small group can then decide which are the best ideas to share when you report back.

- Different people learn in different ways. Some learn best by looking, some learn best by listening, and some learn best by using more active approaches (such as through drama). The units in this book give opportunities to learn in all these ways.

- When you are asked to write an article, leaflet, playscript or poem, you will be given plenty of support. For example, before writing an article yourself, you will see actual examples of newspaper articles. The activities will help you understand exactly how articles are put together, and then you can be far more confident in writing your own article in an effective way.

- At the end of each unit you are asked to think about what you have learned and what the next steps are for you. This will help you make the most of the work you have done through the course of the unit, and help make sure the benefits aren't wasted.

- There is also clear guidance at the end of each unit on how you can move on to higher levels in the future. This means that you can set yourself realistic and achieveable targets to steadily increase your skills in speaking and listening, reading and writing.

- In many places in the book, words are given dictionary definitions, such as the ones below. These are intended to help you understand the word as it is used at that point in the book, but also to help you with the activity you are doing so you can be confident and successful. It's worth having a good look at these, wherever they occur.

WORDS

▲ **best** • *adjective* (superlative of GOOD) most excellent, suitable or desirable.
• *noun* **1** the most desirable quality or result. **2** the greatest effort; one's utmost.
▲ **do one's level best** to do one's very best; to make every effort.
▲ **level** *noun* a stage or degree of progress (e.g. *took exams at an advanced level*).
▲ **pun** *noun* the use of a word or phrase that can be understood in two different ways.

1 Reading for information
Water!

Your focus

The content of this unit is designed to:
- improve your skills in finding information
- increase your skills in reading in different ways.

Your target

By the end of this unit you should be more able to:
- choose the best way of finding information quickly
- choose the best way to read a particular type of text
- take notes efficiently
- write effective information and persuasion aimed at a particular audience.

Your move

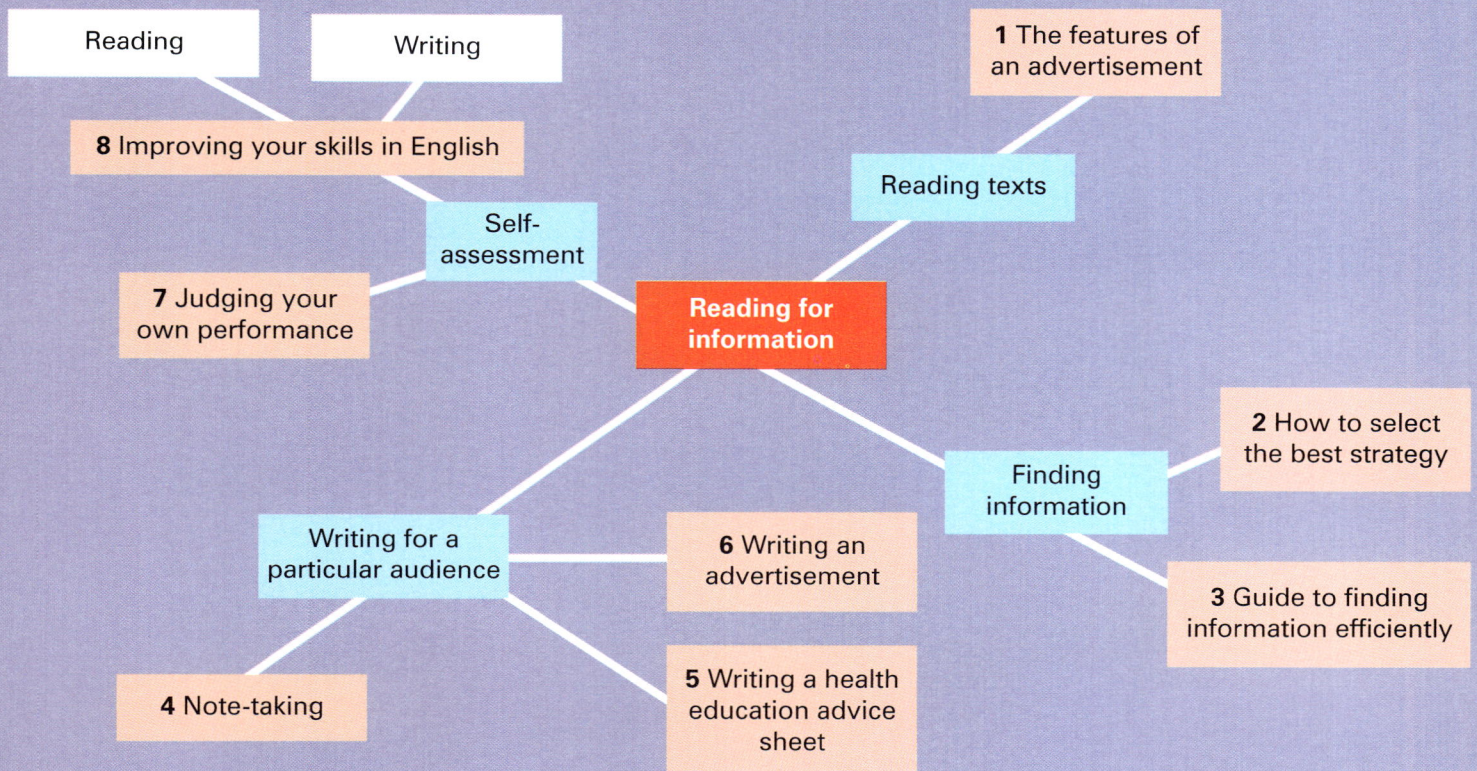

Reading

Writing

8 Improving your skills in English

Self-assessment

7 Judging your own performance

Reading for information

1 The features of an advertisement

Reading texts

2 How to select the best strategy

Finding information

3 Guide to finding information efficiently

Writing for a particular audience

6 Writing an advertisement

4 Note-taking

5 Writing a health education advice sheet

Reading texts

Your car: one ton of metal
A child: flesh and bone

THINK!

1 The features of an advertisement

▶ Look at the advertisement on page 6 and discuss the following questions in your group:

a Who is this advertisement aimed at? How can you tell?

b What effect is this advertisement meant to have?

c Why is there a black background?

d Why is the writing at the top in red?

e Why is the word 'Think!' printed the way it is?

f Why have the words 'ton' and 'metal' been used? (Can you think of any alternatives that would have been more effective?)

g Why have the words 'flesh' and 'bone' been used? (Can you think of any alternatives that would have been more effective?)

h Why have the words 'Your car' been used, rather than 'A car', for example?

i Why have the words 'A child' been used, rather than an alternative?

j What connection is the reader meant to make between the two lines in red?

k How does the way the advertisement is set out encourage the reader to make this connection?

l Do you think this advertisement is effective?

m Where do you think this advertisement might have been displayed?

▶ When you have finished the questions, discuss these points:

a Were you *reading* the advertisement or was it more than just reading?

b Does *reading* include making sense of colour and layout as well as words?

c Look up the word 'read' in your dictionary and see if it includes the skills you used in answering questions **a** to **m**.

ADVICE

▲ Many of the questions **a** to **m** have more than one possible answer.

▲ In your groups, decide on the answer that you think fits the advertisement best.

▲ Make notes on your decisions so you can report back effectively to other groups.

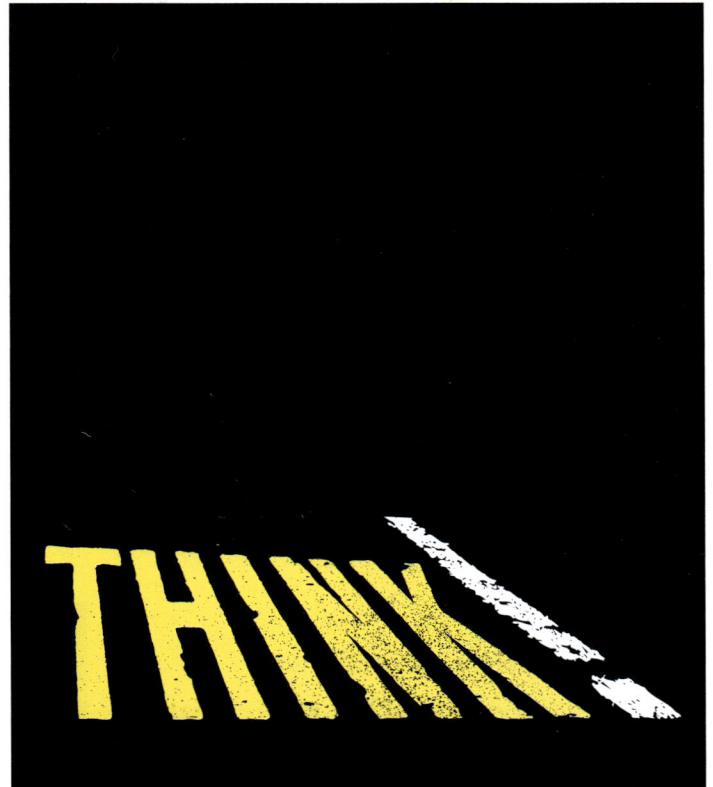

Finding information

You have spent a considerable amount of time exploring in detail how just *twelve words* have been used in an advertisement. Looking at word choice and discussing it is one type of reading. But you don't always read in the same way. You will be asked to read the text for Activity 2 using very different skills. It was published in the *Independent* newspaper in August 2000.

WORDS

▲ **strategy** *noun* a plan or method devised to meet a need.

2 How to select the best strategy

▶ You will be using the newspaper article on water on page 9 to produce a health education advice sheet. This will contain useful information but should also aim to persuade the readers to act differently if they need to.

▶ In pairs, use the article to find answers to the following questions. You will need to be able to tell the rest of the class how you came to find the information. Use the right-hand column of your own notes to remind yourselves.

Question	Answer according to the article	Strategy used to find the right part of the text
How much water should an adult drink a day?		
What health problems may be caused by lack of water?		
How much of the human body is made up of water?		
What is wrong with drinking tea, coffee and soft drinks?		
Who is Jo Jacobius?		
Who wrote *Gut Reaction*?		
Why are the elderly at risk from lack of water?		
Why are children at risk from lack of water?		
What happens to the attention span of a child after drinking water?		

3 Guide to finding information efficiently

▶ Write a five-point guide giving some handy hints on how to find information quickly and efficiently.

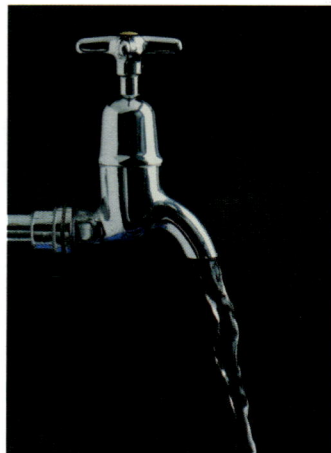

Four pints is good for you. Water, that is

It can cure headaches, indigestion, mood swings, and it aids concentration. And it comes from a tap near you. By **Susannah Prain**

WE ARE all aware that our bodies need water. An adult's daily intake should exceed 1.8 litres, or eight glasses. But do we actually drink enough? Apparently not. Research suggests that only one in ten adults is drinking the optimum amount. The rest of us leave ourselves prone to mood swings, headaches, poor concentration and digestive problems that would take little more than a few glasses of water to solve.

So why aren't we compulsively downing the source of life? In this day of free-range and organic food and juice bars, why aren't we going down to the public house for a few pints of H_2O? Perhaps the answer lies in the fact that it's virtually a free commodity, which renders it a worthless substance. The result is that water becomes overlooked.

Modern lifestyles are partly to blame. Air conditioning can make offices as dry as deserts, and quenching your thirst on caffeine drinks is counter-productive as it will only make dehydration worse.

The human body is made up of approximately 75 per cent water, and it is believed that brain tissue consists of up to 85 per cent water. If we tions of water in our bodies, the results are both physically and mentally detrimental. Ailments include indigestion, constipation and irritability. Water is essential for every physical and chemical process that occurs in the body, it also helps to fight illness, regulates our temperature and moisturises our skin. Refined foods, tea, coffee and soft drinks create a build-up of toxins in our bodies, which water helps to eliminate.

Jo Jacobius, director of the Natural Mineral Water Information Service, says, "Whatever kind of water people choose, whether it be tap or bottled, they should be drinking more. Just because water is clear and tasteless, it doesn't mean that it doesn't contain elements that are beneficial." Ms Jacobius, not surprisingly, recommends drinking natural mineral water, because it is "water as nature intended, and has had nothing added and nothing removed". She states that although tap water is safe to drink, it contains added sodium and fluoride which some people may wish to avoid.

Without sufficient water, Gudrun Jonsson, author of *Gut Reaction*, warns that "waste stays in the system longer and deposits may remain clinging resolutely to the walls of the digestive tract to create a disturbance of one sort or another", which can lead to kidney problems and even gallstones. She claims that "chronic dehydration can be a contributory factor in asthma, high blood pressure, heartburn, indigestion, fatigue, constipation, backache and pains in the joints".

One of the problems, says Dr John Leiper, a research fellow in exercise physiology at Aberdeen University, is that thirst is a poor indicator of how hydrated an individual is. "The danger of water is that it is immediately thirst-quenching and therefore the effects of a dry mouth are instantly refreshed." Dr Leiper warns that this can lead to people not drinking enough water. For example, in an average gym, the plastic cups available are large enough to contain 25 millilitres of water, which is enough to satisfy post-exercise thirst, but would need to be refilled a couple of times in order to rehydrate the body after exercise.

Dr Leiper suggests that the elderly and the young are the most at risk of suffering from dehydration. "Elderly people are often suffering from some form of illness, or living in over-heated buildings, and on both counts should therefore be drinking more water.

"Children are very energetic and therefore need to drink more water, but unfortunately the situation at schools doesn't provide them with the time or opportunity to drink enough fluids. Parents should insist on giving their children a bottle of water to take to school, as research shows that the attention span of a child is increased after drinking more fluids." Dr Leiper maintains that a child's intake of fluids needn't be only water and that a glass of low-calorie squash is just as beneficial. "You have to pander to a child's tastes and many children find the lack of flavour in water renders it boring and tasteless. A study carried out in Canada, where children were given the choice of grape juice or water at break time, concluded that children were more likely to drink the juice because it was a novelty and colourful.

"Even if you drink a lot of water, you don't actually absorb a huge amount of minerals – you receive more from eating fruit and vegetables – so any form of fluid is beneficial." Dr Leiper stresses that losing even two per cent of our body's total water content – one litre – can restrict physical and mental ability to a small extent. Obviously the more you lose, the more detrimental are the effects.

Despite all the fears, Dr Leiper claims that in Britain it is very hard to become seriously dehydrated, unless you become very ill or there is a sudden heatwave, which we all know is completely out of the question this summer.

Only one-in-10 adults drink enough water

Alan Peebles

From the Independent, *24 August 2000*

Writing for a particular audience

WORDS

▲ **attention span**
noun the length
of time during
which a person
is able to
concentrate.
▲ **beneficial**
adjective having
good results or
benefits.
▲ **dehydrate**
intransitive verb
to lose water or
body fluids.
▲ **detrimental**
adjective
harmful,
damaging.
▲ **pander** (to
someone) *verb* to
indulge or gratify
them or their
wishes or tastes.
▲ **toxin** *noun*
a naturally
occurring poison.

4 Note-taking

▶ You are now going to prepare a health education advice sheet on what you have read for one of the following groups of people:

The elderly

or children

or parents

▶ The advice sheet could be called 'Why water is important to humans and especially to [your chosen audience]'.

▶ You will not have the source material when you come to write your piece, so you must use your time wisely to take relevant notes.

▶ You will need to include:
a any details you think they need to know about why water is important to humans.
b any details you think they need to know about why this issue affects them in particular.
c the details you think are most likely to change their behaviour.

▶ You now have five minutes to find any extra information you need. Be prepared to justify why you have selected your chosen details. Use a table like the one below to organise your notes.

Be *selective*! There is far too much detail for your advice sheet in the full article.

Be *precise*! Select the details that are most useful to your target audience.

Be *persuasive*! Choose the facts and figures that are most impressive for your target audience.

What to look for in the article	Your notes
Any details you think they need to know about why water is important to humans	
Any details you think they need to know about why this issue affects them in particular	
The details you think are most likely to change their behaviour	

5   Writing a health education advice sheet

▶ Before starting on your advice sheet, think about the best way you could present your information and ideas.

▶ In making your decisions about the design and content of your advice sheet, you should consider:

   a AUDIENCE: what types of word, what types of sentence and what overall structure are most appropriate for your target audience?

   b TONE: should you be calm and factual, or fun and entertaining? Should you be like a teacher to a pupil, or like a friend to a friend?

   c LAYOUT: what layout of text on the page will make the ideas and information easy to grasp?

   d STRUCTURE: what should come first, in the middle and last to help the reader understand the message clearly?

   e PURPOSE: what is the reason for writing to this audience? (In this case, it is to inform and probably to affect their behaviour in some way.)

▶ Design and write your advice sheet on the importance of water to the elderly/children/parents.

▶ If you wish to illustrate your leaflet, do not spend a long time on this. You could simply draw a box where you want the illustration to go, and write a note to the designer saying what sort of illustration you would like.

> **ADVICE**
>
> ▲ Remember to include some persuasion as well as information in your advice sheet.

6   Writing an advertisement

▶ Look back at the road safety advertisement on page 6. That used just 12 words to get its message across in a powerful way.

▶ Write an advertisement about the importance of water to one of the groups mentioned in Activities 4 and 5 (the elderly, children or parents) using no more than 20 words. Think about audience, tone, layout, structure and purpose as you did for your health education advice sheet.

▶ When you have finished your advertisement, make notes on the differences between your advice leaflet and your advertisement, using those five headings and explaining your decisions.

> **ADVICE**
>
> ▲ It will help if you think where the advertisement might appear, e.g. in a magazine or as a poster. Where would your target group be most likely to see it?
>
> ▲ Spend most of your time on choosing the exact words which will make the greatest impact.
>
> ▲ You can also write notes to a designer for details of pictures, use of colour, choice and size of font and other aspects of design that will help make your advertisement effective for its audience.

Self-assessment

7 Judging your own performance

▶ From the list below:
  a select three points on which you feel you have made the most progress.
  b select one point on which you most need to improve.
  I can read a text closely, commenting on the author's choice of words.
  I can work out why a text has particular features of design and layout.
  I know that I don't have to read every word when searching for information.
  I can cope with words I don't understand by reading on and working out the general meaning.
  I have good strategies for finding information quickly.
  I can take notes which are not too short and not too detailed, and which I can understand a week later.
  I can write an advice sheet suitable for a particular audience.

8 Improving your skills in English

▶ Select one or two skills you need to concentrate on to improve your skills in reading. Then do the same for your writing skills. (The descriptions of levels are a guide, not a rulebook.)

Reading skill	From	To
1 Locate and use information	Level 3	Level 4
2 Begin to use inference and deduction (reading between the lines)	Level 3	Level 4
3 Find and compare information from a range of sources	Level 4	Level 5
4 Use inference and deduction	Level 4	Level 5
5 Identify layers of meaning and comment on their significance and effect	Level 5	Level 6
6 Understand how meaning and information are conveyed in a range of texts	Level 6	Level 7
7 Evaluate how authors achieve their effects through the use of linguistic, structural and presentational devices	Level 7	Above Level 7

Writing skill	From	To
1 Ideas organised appropriately for audience	Level 3	Level 4
2 Full stops, capital letters and question marks used correctly	Level 3	Level 4
3 Words used for their precise meaning	Level 4	Level 5
4 Commas, apostrophes and inverted commas usually used accurately	Level 4	Level 5
5 Style of writing suited to advice sheet and target audience	Level 5	Level 6
6 Ideas organised into paragraphs; a range of punctuation used to clarify meaning	Level 5	Level 6
7 Ideas are organised and coherent	Level 6	Level 7
8 Paragraphing and correct punctuation used to make the ideas coherent and clear to the target audience	Level 6	Level 7
9 Choice of words and grammar enable fine distinctions to be made	Level 7	Above Level 7
10 Clear grasp of the use of punctuation and paragraphing	Level 7	Above Level 7

2 Recognising text types
Endurance

Your focus

The content of this unit is designed to:
- develop your skills in reading different types of writing
- help you to write convincingly in a range of forms.

Your target

By the end of this unit you should be more able to:
- recognise by whom and to whom a text has been written
- read a variety of texts with greater understanding
- take notes efficiently
- write a variety of text types more effectively.

Your move

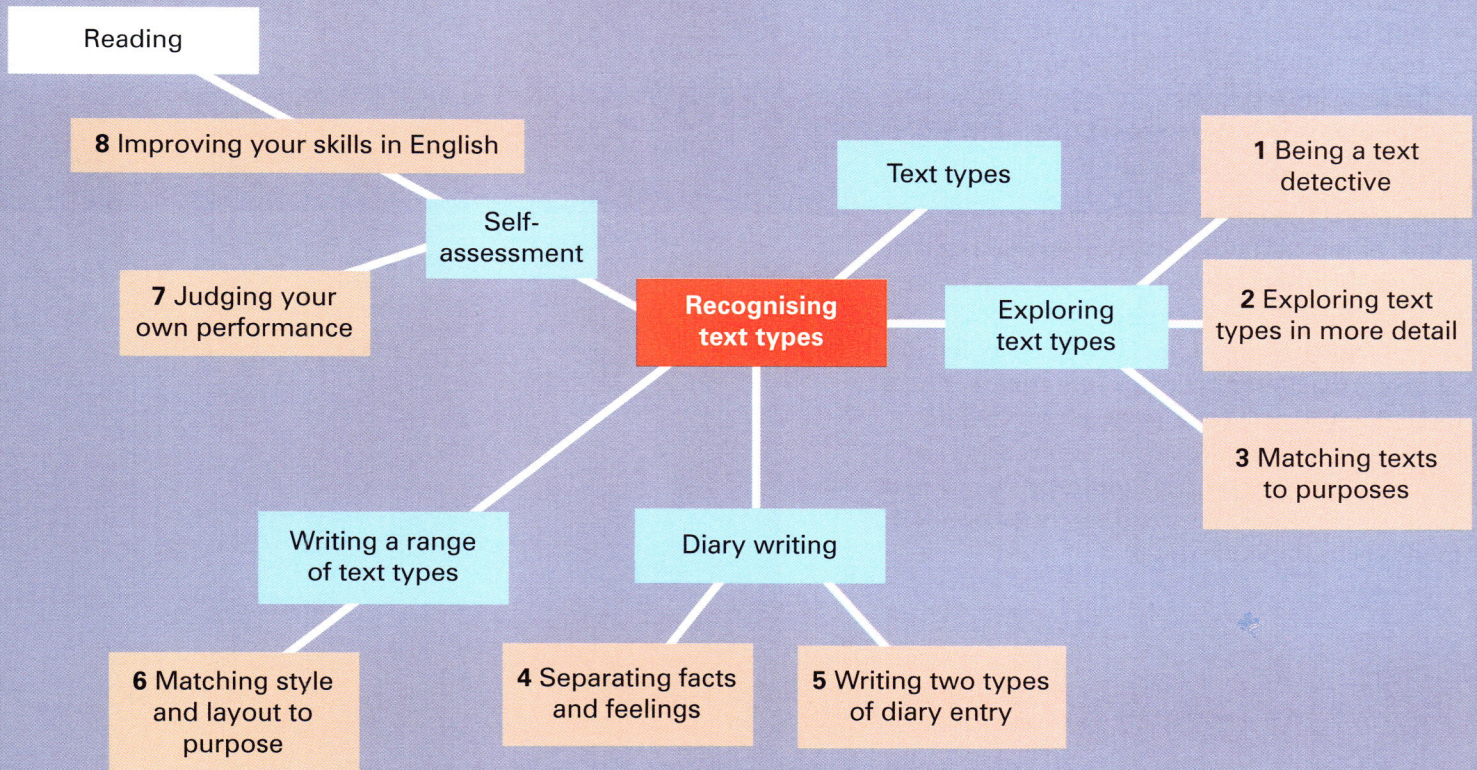

Reading

8 Improving your skills in English

Self-assessment

Text types

1 Being a text detective

7 Judging your own performance

Recognising text types

Exploring text types

2 Exploring text types in more detail

3 Matching texts to purposes

Writing a range of text types

Diary writing

6 Matching style and layout to purpose

4 Separating facts and feelings

5 Writing two types of diary entry

Text types

Over the course of your study in English, you read and write a whole variety of texts. It helps you to **read** a text if you know what kind of text it is, and the only way you can **write** a text effectively is if you know what is special about that particular type of text.

The main types of *fiction* you study in English are:

- drama or plays (see Units 7 and 10). (Remember that a soap on television is a play.) You will also be studying plays by Shakespeare
- novels and short stories (see Units 3 and 9)
- poems (see Unit 5).

Non-fiction, which you also study in English, includes the following:

- information texts – giving the reader some facts about a situation, etc. (see Units 2, 4 and 8)
- recounts – giving an account of what happened (see Unit 2)
- explanation – giving the reasons why something happens (see Unit 2)
- instructions – describing how something is done
- persuasion – trying to influence the reader's thinking or behaviour (see Units 2 and 4)
- discursive writing – presenting both sides of an argument (see Unit 6).

This unit is designed to help you recognise some of the different types of text you will be exploring in the later units so you are more familiar with what to expect.

On pages 15 to 21 you will see a collection of texts (labelled **A** to **I**) on one theme. Use a table like the one here to help you decide what links all these texts. As you read more, you will find you understand more – not just about the text you are reading, but about all the texts in the collection.

▶ What is the connection between all these texts?
▶ Find as many links as you can. The first link has been completed for you.

Detail in...	Text	Link to detail in...	Text
Antarctica	A	Antarctic continent	B

Geography

Continent

Also known as
Antarctique
Antarktis

Total area
14,000,000 square kilometres
5,400,000 square miles

Maximum elevation
5,139 metres
16,860 feet

Average elevation
2,000 metres
8,000 feet

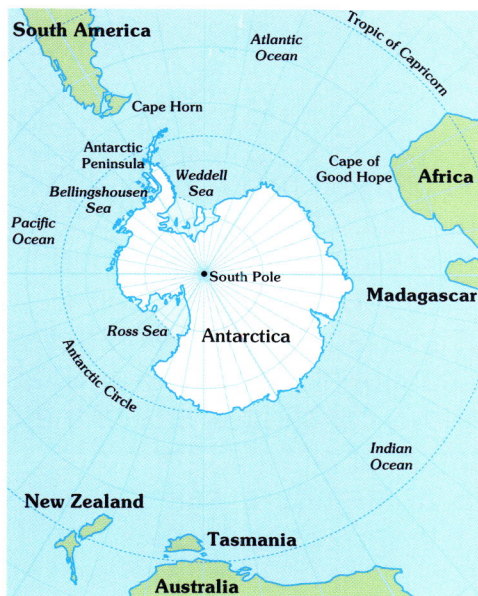

Ice-bound Antarctica is inhabited primarily by penguins and seals, with a few invertebrates such as mites and ticks, which are the only land animals that can tolerate the low temperatures. The rich Antarctica marine life includes krill, a shrimp-like organism that is a food source for the large numbers of whales in the surrounding waters. Antarctica has no trees, flowering plants or grasses—vegetation is limited to about 350 species, mostly lichens, mosses, and algae.

As strange as it seems, Antarctica can be classified as a true desert, for in the interior the average annual precipitation is only about 50 millimetres (2 inches). The average temperature on the continent is -50°C (-58°F), and the land is swept by strong, sometimes hurricane-force winds. Blizzards are frequent, when winds pick up previously deposited snow and move it from place to place. The lowest temperature ever recorded on earth, -89.2°C (-128.6°F), was measured at Vostok Station on 21 July 1983. The icy land mass and severely cold temperatures have so far limited human habitation.

In addition to being the coldest, windiest, and driest continent, Antarctica is also the highest, with an average elevation of about 2,000 metres (8,000 feet).

B

PBS Home   Search   Programs A-Z   TV Schedules   Shop   Station Finder

NOVA Home | Site Map | E-mail

NOVA PBS

ONLINE ADVENTURE

Sponsored by MORGAN STANLEY DEAN WITTER

Shackleton
Home

Shackleton's expedition

NOVA's expedition

Surviving

Navigating

Dispatches

Classroom

Site map

1914   1916   1915   Timeline

When he left South Georgia Island on December 5, 1914 in his bid to be the first to cross the Antarctic continent, Ernest Shackleton had no idea that the next bit of land he touched (save for remote Elephant Island) would be that very same South Georgia - a year and a half later and after having not so much as set foot on the Antarctic continent. The story of what happened in between, outlined below, constitutes one of the most stupendous polar survival sagas of all time. For more specifics on the expedition and its 28 members, see the dispatches and Meet Shackleton's team, respectively.

December 5
Departs Grytviken whaling station, South Georgia - last time crew would touch land for 497 days

1915

Heeled over by the unrelenting force of the pack ice, the *Endurance* awaits a splintery end.

January 10
First sighting of Antarctic continent

January 18
Endurance becomes beset in the pack ice

February 24
Shackleton orders halt to ship routine

May 1
Sun vanishes for season, not to reappear for four months

June 22
Crew celebrates Midwinter's Day with a feast

August 27
Frank Hurley takes famous nighttime photos of *Endurance*

September 2
Pressure ice makes the *Endurance*, according to Perce Blackborow, "literally [jump] into the air and [settle] on its beam."

October 27
At 5 p.m., Shackleton gives order to abandon the *Endurance*

November 21
With a single cry of "She's going, boys!" Shackleton and his crew watch *Endurance* sink

🖹 | Updated November 2000

C

MEN WANTED: FOR HAZARDOUS JOURNEY. SMALL WAGES, BITTER COLD, LONG MONTHS OF COMPLETE DARKNESS, CONSTANT DANGER, SAFE RETURN DOUBTFUL. HONOUR AND RECOGNITION IN CASE OF SUCCESS. SIR ERNEST SHACKLETON.

D

We now had twenty-two and a half hours of daylight, and throughout the day we watched the threatening advance of the ice floes. At 6.45 p.m. the ship sustained heavy pressure in a dangerous position. The onslaught was almost irresistible. The ship groaned and quivered as her starboard quarter was forced against the floe. The ship was twisted and actually bent by the stresses. She began to leak dangerously at once.

The attack of the ice is illustrated roughly in the appended diagram. The shaded portions represent the pool, covered with new ice which afforded no support to the ship, and the arrows indicate the direction of the pressure exercised by the thick floes and pressure-ridges.

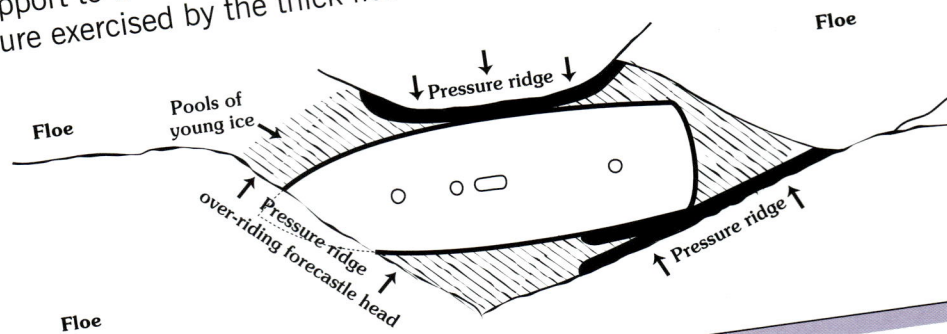

E

There was endless speculation as to where and when the ship would be released from the floe and be once more free to take us back to civilization. Never for a moment did it occur to any of us that what actually happened would happen.

There was little danger; so strongly was she built, with twelve inch square beams athwartships at four foot intervals on every deck; it would take more than mere ice-pressure to shiver her timbers, that is how we all felt. I am glad only that I witnessed it. Metro-Goldwyn with a ten million dollar film could not have done it better, with us and the dogs helplessly looking on, wondering what was going to happen next. After two days of 'all hands to the pumps' pumping a losing battle with the icy water coming in from the ship's dislodged stern-post, life on board became so dangerous that the Boss gave the order, 'Abandon ship', oft heard in ship's 'stations' for exercise, but the only time I have ever heard it given in earnest. Therewith the pumps were abandoned and all hands turned to like frenzied demons shifting overboard and on to the floe the masses of equipment and provision that had been expressly set aside for just such an occasion.

There were the dogs that had to be attended to, the three boats to be lowered on the floe, tents, sleeping bags, boxes by the hundred and the two aero sledges for the sake of their sledge portions. At last all was done. The Boss was standing on the top of the gangway as each of us passed over the side.

F

Severe pressure on and off all morning, getting very bad in afternoon. Ship lifted bodily but with a bad list to starboard. Ice coming aft pressed against rudder and carried away both stern posts. All hope abandoned, leak increasing rapidly. All remaining gear put ashore as far as possible and temporary camp made. Had dinner on ship at night but water already coming into Ritz.

Pitched our tents and turned in about 10 p.m. but pressure continued and our floe cracked about 11 p.m. and we had to shift camp.

A terrible night, with the ship outlined dark against the sky and the worst of the pressure against her and all around seeming like the cries of a living creature. Very cold and miserable time. Temperature well below zero.

G

"Endurance" Abandoned.

OCTOBER, 1915.

First night on floe 1182½ / 1186½

300   BILLS DUE WITH GRACE.
30 Days—Nov. 29.
60 Days—Dec. 29.
90 Days—Jan. 28.

22½ h. deg.
10th Month
light

Bar 29.89
air min — 8.5
0

S. 69.5'
W. 51°32'22"
N 25° W 4 m

27 WEDNESDAY [300—65]

Gentle SSE to SSW breeze & clear weather no land visible for 20 miles Pressure throughout day, increasing to terrific force at 4 P.M., heaving stern up smashing rudder, rudderpost & stern-post. Decks breaking up. 7 P. Ship too dangerous to live in we are forced to abandon her. Water overmastering pumps & coming up to engine fires. Draw fires & let down steam.

Men & dogs camp on floe, but having to shift camp twice with floe cracking & smashing underfoot get little sleep.

We have 2 pole tents & 3 hoop tents. No 1 In charge Sir E. Hudson, 4 Hurley & James take the small pole tent. The 8 forward hands take the large hoop tent. 3 Wild, Wordie, Macneish, & McIlroy take one small hoop tent N° 2 Crean takes charge in charge of N° 4 with Hussey, Marston, Cheetham. I take charge of N° 5 with Greenstreet, Lees, Clark, Kerr, Rickinson Macklin & Blackboro from the fore-hands (a very decent young lad)

The ship was not abandoned one hour too soon, for shortly after we had camped on the floe we could hear the crushing & smashing up of her beams & timbers & subsequent examination of her showed that only 6 cabins aboard had not been pierced by floes & blocks of ice. The whole of the "fo'castle" & "Ritz" were submerged, the Ward-room & every one of the starboard cabins were driven in by ice. It is a heartbreaking sound to hear such a gallant & stout little ship being remorselessly crushed by the pack after her long brave fight against it. The petrol cases stacked on the fore deck were driven by the floe clean thro the wall of the house into the Wardroom, & a picture of (the King?) had been pushed right across the W'room without damage or even cracking the glass.

"Endurance" crushed & abandoned after drifting Point to Point Drift
N. 38° W. 573 miles in 281 days.   Total drift thro all Obs⁰ Positions = 1186½ miles.

Party on Floe 24.X.15. from Pos 69°5' S. 51°32'22" W.

H

October 27th. A most exciting day – perhaps the most exciting of our Expedition. I was taking a little snooze in the fo'c'sle with Bakewell and How shortly after teatime, when Wild stuck his head around the door and woke us. 'She's going, boys,' he said. 'I think it's time to get off.' Bakewell and How jumped up from their beds, and I stretched where I was on Blackborow's. 'Take my kit, will you?' Bakewell said to How. 'I'll get Chippy. Come on, Mrs Chips,' he said to me, and gently picked me up and tucked me under his arm. I was still somewhat asleep as we hurried up top, and so found everything rather confusing, with all my shipmates milling around the deck and going over the rail, and the dogs being unchained from their kennels. Suddenly I realized that Bakewell was taking me over the rail! I won't say I was panicky but I was suddenly very concerned that he might not understand the exact nature and character of the dogs with respect to a sailor such as myself... I began to struggle and he tried to hold me more tightly, talking all the time, but I had my eye on the dogs and wasn't entirely listening. 'Ow!' he exclaimed. 'Blast it! Chippy! Ow!' Then, 'Look! Here's your mate. Now everything will be all right.'... My mate came striding over to us and taking me firmly around the middle... began to smooth down my fluffed-up fur... Then holding me very firmly indeed, with one hand on my scruff, he strode towards the gangway. 'Have a last look, Chippy,' he said. 'We none of us will be back here again.'

I

SIR E. SHACKLETON'S STORY.

750-MILE JOURNEY TO GET HELP.

TERRIBLE EXPERIENCES IN THE ICE PACK.

Having left South Georgia in December, 1914, the Endurance entered the pack ice and forced her way for 1,000 miles through icebergs. But abnormal circumstances now intervened. Summer conditions were non-existent. The Endurance was beset in the ice and never got free.

On October 16 1915, in the space of 10 seconds, heavy pressure forced the ship right on to the ice, and on October 27 the end came. Icebergs pierced the ship, the water overmastered the pumps, the main deck breaking upwards. All hands took to the ice – the position was extremely serious.

Exploring text types

1 Being a text detective

► How much can you work out about these texts? You may find that a piece of information in one text will help you answer the questions on another piece of text. You can't give exact answers to all the questions.

► When considering the type of text, decide whether each text is fiction or non-fiction. If it is non-fiction, decide which of these categories it fits most closely:

a Information – giving the reader some facts about a situation, etc.
b Recount – telling a story of what happened.
c Explanation – giving the reasons why something happened.
d Persuasion – trying to influence the reader's thinking or behaviour.

► Use a table like this to organise your ideas.

ADVICE

▲ You will need to write down the reasons for any decisions you make so you can report back to the other groups afterwards.
▲ One member of your group should make a note of the clues you find which lead you to your decisions.

Text	Who wrote it?	Who to?	When?	Why? + type of text
A				
B				
C				
D				
E				
F				
G				
H				
I				

2 Exploring text types in more detail

▶ For this activity, you will be concentrating on just four of the texts (**A**, **C**, **D** and **F**).

▶ Find an example of each of the features mentioned and make a note of them for later discussion. Use a different example in each case.

▶ Organise your ideas in a table like the one below.

3 Matching texts to purposes

▶ Which would be the best text to use if you were a scientist looking for accurate information?
▶ Which would be the best text to use to help you prepare a filmscript?
▶ Which would be the best text to use to give a dramatic reading of the events of that day?
▶ Which text lets you know most about the feelings of those on board on that day?
▶ Which text tells you most about the person writing it?
▶ Which is your favourite text and why?

Be ready to explain your choices to the other groups.

Information text: typical features	Example in text A
Use of a heading to say what this part of the text is about	
Opening definition of some sort	
Present tense	
Use of facts and figures	
Use of some sort of illustration to add information/break up the text	
Recount text: typical features	**Example in text F**
Chronological order (events retold in correct time sequence)	
Paragraphs used to show change of place or time	
Past tense	
Words chosen to express feelings	
Use of imagery, e.g. simile	
Explanation text: typical features	**Example in text D**
Text refers to a diagram to help the reader understand	
Text is used to explain how to understand the diagram	
Past tense for past events	
Use of some technical terms	
Persuasion text: typical features	**Example in text C**
Use of particular font for impact	
Use of humour to get point across	
Short sentences for effect	
Parts of sentence missing	
Use of powerful words to influence reader	

Diary writing

4 Separating facts and feelings

▶ Some diary writers concentrate on facts and figures. Others use their diaries to record their thoughts and feelings.

▶ Using texts **F** and **G** only, write down:
a ten details giving facts and figures.
b ten details giving thoughts and feelings.

▶ The following extract is from the same diary as text **H**, but three days earlier. Read it through carefully.

October 24th. Calm, bright morning. Breakfast of seal. After checking that all the fires were going well, went up top for my watch. The ice was moving a great deal, making it difficult for me to make clear sightings. Observed as the ice rose up in places and burst open, just as if a whale had smashed through it, only there wasn't one. Noted the onset of inclement weather by tingling in tips of whiskers and hastened below, settling in wardroom on my accustomed chair. An hour later, my shipmates returned for lunch, covered with snow. 'We should have come in when you did, Chippy,' said Cheetham. 'How does Chippy *always* know when bad weather's coming?' After lunch, took a short break in the potato pot until teatime, and then again at dinner. Joined my shipmates in the wardroom for dinner, supplementing my own meal with a little something here and there, to help ward off the cold. Was just going to join my mate on his constitutional stroll when we were all violently shaken and an odd and very unpleasant screaming noise arose from the ship. My shipmates froze, then rushed above. Left alone, I first examined my shipmates' bowls, just in case they had wasted anything, then decided to join them up top. Found everyone in great disarray, running around and pointing and exclaiming at the ice. Many of my shipmates looked pale and shaky, rather like they do when they are going to be seasick, leading me to wonder if we were going to be under way again. Joined Macklin, the Skipper and Hussey at the rail. 'I don't believe I have ever before been made so aware of the colossal forces of Nature,' said Macklin in a solemn voice. Leaping to the rail, I saw that all the ice was rippling, like a great but slowed-down wave coming towards us. Checked ice intently for seals, but saw none. I have always known about the 'colossal forces of Nature,' i.e., rainstorms that soak my fur, and all the shifting seas, so I was not surprised. I thought all proper Explorers knew this. Suddenly my mate ran past us, followed by the Boss. 'Come on, Chippy, you shouldn't be up here,' said Hussey, and scooping me up he accompanied me fore, where we found Blackborow. My fur was a little on end with all the confusion and the screaming of the ship and so forth, and it was very nice to have Blackborow stroke it down. He and I went below to the fo'c'sle, where I was placed upon his spare sweater. 'Best stay here, Chippy,' he said. 'No one knows what's happening from one moment to the next. You take charge of things here.' Kneaded his sweater with my paws, settling down after he left. It is the same old pattern of noise, shaking and then complete muddle. Dozed off and was awoken by Bakewell and How coming in and flopping down on their bunks as if tired. Woke again to find Bakewell and How gone, and Vincent and McCarthy flopping down on their beds. Speculating that this might go on all night, I burrowed more tightly into Blackborow's sweater, so as to ensure that I would not continue to be disturbed.

5 Writing two types of diary entry

▶ Some diaries, as we have seen, are mainly informative, whereas others can express the individual's inner thoughts and feelings. You are going to write two contrasting diary entries, making them sound as if they are actual diaries written by two different people on board the *Endurance*. They are each writing their diary entry for 24 October.

▶ Write down five details that you think are probably true facts from Chippy's diary entry for 24 October.

▶ Write down ten details that help you work out what Chippy's shipmates are thinking and feeling.

▶ In one diary entry, use the five factual details and write the diary as if written by a scientist who wants to record the facts of the expedition for future generations. You may be able to work out some extra facts which are mixed up with opinion in Chippy's account.

▶ In the second diary entry, record the person's thoughts and feelings. This person is more interested in remembering the interesting and exciting moments of the journey.

Writing a range of text types

6 Matching style and layout to purpose

▶ Choose a topic on which you can write a range of text types. For example, think of television programmes in which a number of people are put in a confined area or on an island for a number of days/months, with viewers kept up to date with how individuals are coping.

▶ Aim for short sharp examples of each of the following:
  a Information: write the entry for the *Radio Times* which will inform the viewing public that this programme is on. Do not include any commentary, but simply state the facts.
  b Recount: write the account of one person who took part, halfway through the experience, either as a diary or as a letter to a friend.
  c Explanation: explain how the programme will work, as if you are explaining it in writing to volunteers.
  d Persuasion: write a suitable advertisement encouraging volunteers to apply to take part in a new programme of this type. Say what publication the advertisement will appear in.
  e Discursive writing: write a review of the programme after the first edition has been broadcast, pointing out its strengths and weaknesses. Name the publication in which it will appear. (Alternatively, this could be 'persuasion', only giving one side of the argument.)

▶ Explain how you used language, layout, etc. differently to suit each audience and purpose.

Self-assessment

7 Judging your own performance

▶ From the list below:

a select three points on which you feel you have made the most progress.

b select one point on which you most need to improve.

I can recognise the difference between fiction and non-fiction.

I can recognise a text which gives information.

I can recognise a text which is mainly recount.

I can recognise a text which gives an explanation.

I can recognise a text which is designed for persuasion.

I can write a diary entry which is mainly factual.

I can write a diary entry which expresses thoughts and feelings.

I can write a diary entry which looks and reads like a diary entry.

8 Improving your skills in English

▶ Select one or two skills you need to concentrate on to improve your skills in reading. (The descriptions of levels are a guide, not a rulebook.)

	Reading skill	From	To
1	Show understanding of significant events and characters	Level 3	Level 4
2	Select essential points and use inference and deduction	Level 4	Level 5
3	Refer to aspects of language, structure and theme to justify opinions about texts	Level 5	Level 6
4	Select and synthesise a range of information from a variety of sources	Level 6	Level 7
5	Select and analyse information and ideas, and comment on how these are conveyed in different texts	Level 7	Above Level 7

3 Responding to fiction
Goodnight Mister Tom

Your focus

The content of this unit is designed to:
- develop your skills in reading different types of texts, especially fiction
- help you understand the choices authors make.

Your target

By the end of this unit you should be more able to:
- understand the techniques authors use to create characters and places
- read between the lines effectively
- recognise the choices authors make (e.g. which words they choose) and the effect these choices have.

Your move

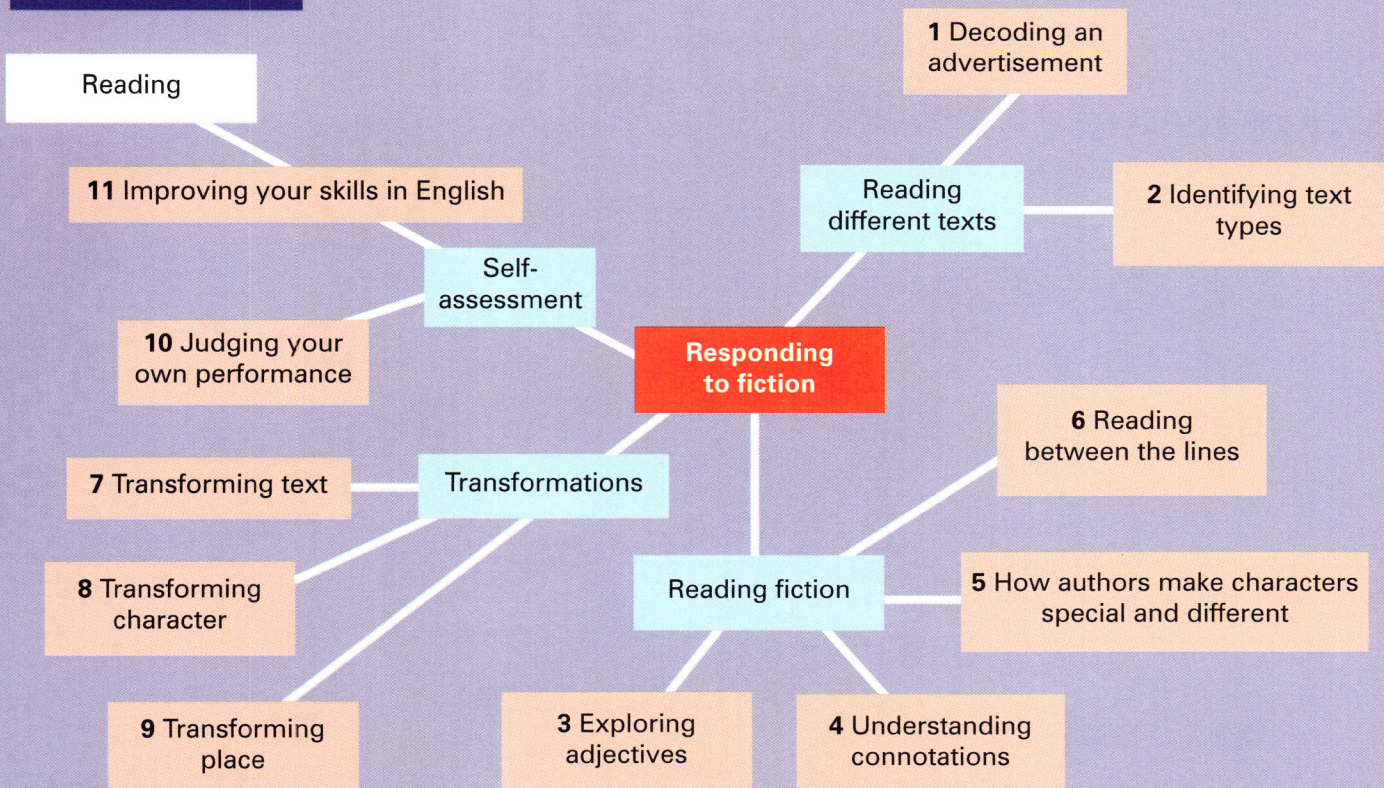

Reading

11 Improving your skills in English

Self-assessment

10 Judging your own performance

7 Transforming text

Transformations

8 Transforming character

9 Transforming place

Responding to fiction

1 Decoding an advertisement

Reading different texts

2 Identifying text types

6 Reading between the lines

Reading fiction

5 How authors make characters special and different

3 Exploring adjectives

4 Understanding connotations

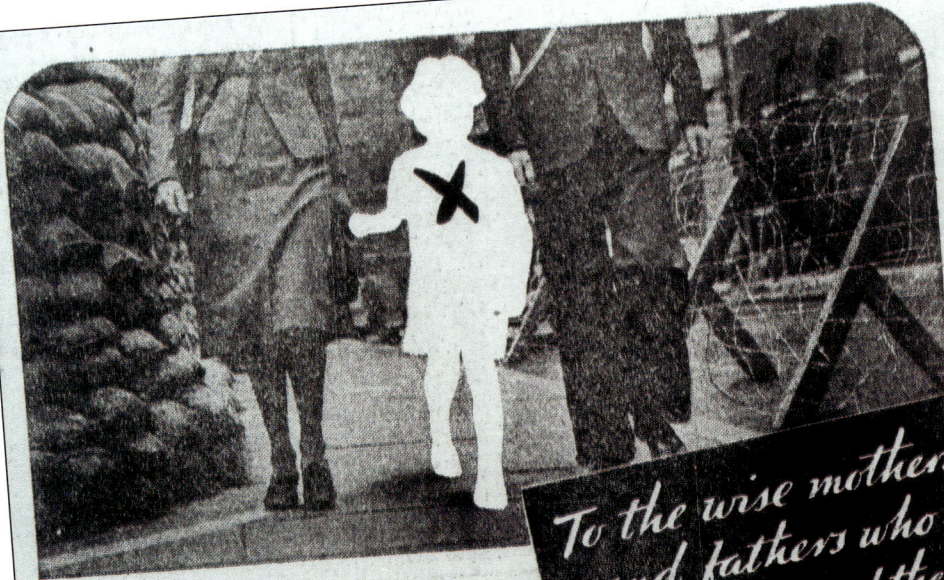

To the wise mothers and fathers who have registered their children for evacuation

The time has come ! You have proved your devotion to your children's welfare by registering them under the Ministry of Health evacuation scheme. You took your chance. Other parents will envy you. Your children have a place of greater safety to go to, thanks to your foresight. Every day now thousands of children are travelling comfortably to the pleasant, homely billets provided for them in the West of England. It is sad to say goodbye for a while. All the more honour to you who prefer that pang of parting to the risk of a maimed or shattered life for your children. Evacuation from London of children *already* registered to places of greater safety is now proceeding. Friendly homes are waiting in the West.

. . . if your children are registered, **see to it that they go to the assembly point about which you have been notified.**

From the Star, *17 June 1940*

Reading different texts

1 **Decoding an advertisement**

▶ Look closely at the advertisement on page 28.
▶ Discuss each of the following questions in your group, making notes on your reasons so you can explain your decision to the other groups:

  a Who is the advertisement aimed at (the audience)?
  b What is the purpose of the advertisement?
  c What is the adjective used to describe the mothers and fathers in the white writing on a black background?
  d Why are they described like this?
  e What words are used to make the mothers and fathers feel good about themselves in the rest of the text?
  f Why are these words chosen?
  g Can you work out what is the 'carrot' and what is the 'stick' in the advertisement?
  h Where does the advertisement admit there will be problems?
  i Why does it admit there will be problems?
  j Why do you think there is a black cross on a white silhouette of a child in the top picture, and a black cross against the sky in the bottom picture?
  k What other differences do you notice about the two pictures, as far as you can tell?
  l Do you think the advertisement gives a fair idea of what children could expect when they went to their new homes? Comment on any words in the advertisement which try to persuade, but also comment on the lower picture.

WORDS

▲ **carrot** *noun* something offered as an incentive.
▲ **stick** *noun* the threat of punishment as a means of obtaining compliance.

2 Identifying text types

▶ Extracts **A** to **F** below have been taken from various sources. Work out which one comes from which source. Plot your findings on a table like the one at the bottom of this page.

▶ Try to explain what it is about the way each extract is written that tells you this.

▶ You will need to be ready to explain to those in other groups exactly why you have come to your conclusions.

ADVICE

Advice on what to look for:
▲ Audience – e.g. 'I am speaking to you...'; 'If your children are registered...'.
▲ Content – e.g. '10 Downing Street'; 'the starting point of the Second World War'.
▲ Length – e.g. 'Poland Invaded!'.
▲ Punctuation – e.g. 'THOUSANDS' written in capitals.
▲ Tense – e.g. 'I am speaking to you...' (present tense); 'Thousands of children are still travelling...' (present tense); 'Mr Bush was seating the small children...' (past tense).

A I am speaking to you from the Cabinet Room at 10 Downing Street. This morning the British Ambassador in Berlin handed the German Government a final note stating that unless we heard from them by eleven o'clock that they were prepared at once to withdraw their troops from Poland, a state of war would exist between us.

B If your children are registered, see to it that they go to the assembly point about which you have been notified.

C Poland Invaded!

D The five of them went into the hall together. The blackout curtains which were rolled neatly above the windows stood out starkly against the light green walls and wooden skirting boards. Mr Bush was seating the small children cross-legged on the polished wooden floor.

F What is usually considered the starting point of the Second World War is the German invasion of Poland in September 1939. From then until Pearl Harbor in December 1941 it was really a European war.

E THOUSANDS of London children are still travelling into the Western Counties, but those who arrived in their new homes on Thursday are settling down already like old soldiers.

Sources

1 Advertisement.
2 History textbook for secondary school pupils.
3 Newspaper article.
4 Novel.
5 Placard outside newsagent's shop.
6 Speech by Mr Chamberlain, Prime Minister.

Extract	Source number	How can you tell which it is? Look at the type of words used and who you think they were aimed at
A		
B		
C		
D		
E		
F		

Reading fiction

③ Exploring adjectives

▶ Read the following description from Michelle Magorian's *Goodnight Mister Tom*, in which Tom is thinking about Willie, the evacuee who is staying in his house.

> The tales he had heard about evacuees didn't seem to fit Willie. 'Ungrateful' and 'wild' were the adjectives he had heard used or just plain 'homesick'. He was quite unprepared for this timid, sickly little specimen.

▶ For each adjective, explain how you can tell if the person using that word is sympathetic to evacuees/Willie or not. Use a table like the one below.

Adjective used	Is the person using the adjective sympathetic to evacuees/Willie or not?
ungrateful	If a person calls evacuees 'ungrateful' it suggests they are not sympathetic to evacuees. It suggests they think evacuees should be more grateful for the home, food, etc. they are being given.
wild	
homesick	Tom thinks Willie is 'homesick'. This suggests Tom is (sympathetic/unsympathetic) because...
timid	
sickly	
little	

▶ Do you think Tom had believed the 'tales' about evacuees before Willie arrived? Why do you think that?
▶ Does this description tell you more about Tom than Willie, or more about Willie than Tom?

④ Understanding connotations

▶ Each word we use has a dictionary definition that tells us what that word means, e.g. 'home' = a place where you live. However, most words have connotations as well. These are the ideas that the word suggests to you – its hidden associations. For example, the word 'home' might have connotations like these for some people: warmth, acceptance, relaxation. Words may have different connotations for different people. For Willie, home will certainly not have these positive connotations.
▶ Words with negative connotations are sometimes called **snarl** words.
▶ Words with positive connotations are sometimes called **purr** words.
▶ Read the following two descriptions of Sammy, Tom's collie dog. In the first extract, Willie has been watching a squirrel when the dog appears. The second takes place inside the house.

A loud sharp barking suddenly disturbed the silence. The squirrel leapt and disappeared. Willie sprang to his feet, hopping on one leg and gasping at the mixture of numbness and pins and needles in the other. A small black-and-white collie ran around the tree and into the leaves. It stopped in front of him and jumped up into the air. Willie was more petrified of the dog than he had been of the squirrel.

5

'Them poisonous dogs,' he heard his mother's voice saying inside him. 'One bite from them muts and you're dead. They got 'orrible diseases in 'em.'

....

' 'E won't harm you,' said Tom. ' 'E's a spry ole thing, but he's soft as butter, ent you, ole boy?' and he knelt down and ruffled his fur. Sammy snuggled up between his knees and licked his face. 'See,' said Tom, ' 'e's very friendly.' Willie tried to smile. 'You want to learn somethin' wot'll make him happy?' He nodded. 'Hold one of yer hands out, palm up, like that,' and he showed the inside of his rough brown hand. Willie copied him. 'That's so he knows you ent going to harm him, see. Now, hold it out towards him and tickle his chest.' Willie leaned nervously forward and touched Sammy's fur. 'That's the idea. You jest keep doin' that.'

Willie stroked him. His fur felt silky and soft. Sammy gave his fingers a long lick.

' 'E likes you, see. When he licks you that's his way of sayin' "I likes you and you makes me happy".'

▶ Writers like Michelle Magorian make their writing more interesting by using a range of adjectives, precisely chosen for particular effects. Write down the adjectives you can find to describe Sammy, Tom's collie dog, from the extract given. Note down if that makes the dog appear:
  ● better (positive connotation)
  ● no better or worse (neutral connotation)
  ● worse (negative connotation).
▶ Use a table like the one below.

Line	Type of description	Adjective used	Connotation: positive, neutral or negative
1	Volume of bark		
1	Kind of noise of bark		
3	Size of dog		
3–4	Colour of dog		
7	Willie's mother's description of all dogs		
9	Character		
9	Age		
9	Character		
11	Character		
18	Description of fur		
18	Description of fur		

▶ Is there a pattern to the positive and negative connotations? Give reasons for any patterns you find.
▶ Explain what the pattern tells you about the author's presentation of the characters.

5 How authors make characters special and different

▶ The author, Michelle Magorian, makes both Mrs Beech (Willie's mother) and Tom Oakley use non-standard English.

▶ Write the standard English version of each of the examples in a table like the one below.

▶ Explain why you think the author uses non-standard English in each case.

▶ You may find it helpful to match up each example to one of these possible reasons, adding more reasons where necessary.

a Showing how they actually pronounce words.

b Showing they use non-standard grammar.

c Showing they don't pronounce every letter in some words.

d Showing how people talk in that local area.

Line	Non-standard English	Standard English	What the author may want to show by using non-standard English
7	Them		
8	'orrible		
8	'em		
9	'E		
9	ole		
10	ent you		
12	somethin'		
12	wot'll		
13	yer		
17	jest		
20	I likes		
21	you makes		

6 Reading between the lines

▶ In these three extracts from *Goodnight Mister Tom* you are not directly told what Willie and Zach are thinking most of the time. But the author gives plenty of clues about their thoughts and feelings.

▶ Make a note of those words that tell you most about Zach's thoughts and feelings.

▶ Make a note of those words that tell you most about Willie's thoughts and feelings. Willie, Tom and the Fletchers are building an Anderson shelter.

When the trench was completed Willie sat on the grass to watch the others fix the Anderson shelter inside it. Sammy lay by his feet. The six steel sheets were inserted into the two widest sides of the trench and bolted together at the top, forming a curved tunnel.

....

'William,' said Tom after the Fletchers had left. 'I'm afraid we ent quite finished yet. We jest got to cover this with earth. Got any strength left?'

Willie felt exhausted but he was determined to keep going. He nodded.

Between them they started to cover the shelter until it was time for Tom to leave for a meeting in the village hall.

'Don't carry on fer long,' he said as he swung the back gate behind him, but Willie continued to pile the earth on, levelling it down with his hands. It was exciting to see the glinting steel slowly disappear under its damp camouflage. He was so absorbed in his task that he didn't notice dusk approaching. His hands and fingernails were filthy, his face and legs were covered in muck, his clothes were sodden and he was glorying in the wetness of it all. He was in the middle of smoothing one piece of earth when a shadow fell across his hands. He looked up quickly and there, half-silhouetted in the twilight, stood the wiry, curly-haired boy he had seen at the Post Office.

....

'Hello!' he said brightly, grasping Willie's hand. There was a loud squelching of mud as he shook it.

'Sorry!' gasped Willie in embarrassment.

The strange boy grinned and wiped it on the seat of his shorts. 'You're William Beech, aren't you?' Willie nodded. 'Pleased to meet you. I'm Zacharias Wrench.'

'Oh,' said Willie.

'Yes, I know. It's a mouthful, isn't it? My parents have a cruel sense of humour. I'm called Zach for short.'

The strange boy's eyes seemed to penetrate so deeply into Willie's that he felt sure he could read his thoughts. He averted his gaze, and began hurriedly to cover the Anderson again.

'I say, can I help? I'd like to.'

Willie was quite taken aback at being asked.

'I'm rather good at it, actually,' he continued proudly. 'I've given a hand at the creation of several. I wouldn't mess it up.'

'Yeh,' replied Willie quietly, 'if you want.'

'Thanks. I say,' he said as he dumped a handful of earth on the side of the shelter. 'I'll show you around. Do you like exploring?'

Willie shrugged his shoulders. 'I dunno.'

'Is it your first visit to the country?' But before Willie could reply the boy was already chattering on. 'It's not mine exactly. I've had odd holidays with friends and my parents but this is the first time I've actually sort of *lived* in the country. I've read books that are set in the country and, of course, poems, and I've lived in towns *near* the country and gone into the country on Sundays or when there was no school.' He stopped and there was a moment of silence as they carried on working. 'You've not been here long, have you?' he asked after a while. Willie shook his head. 'Else I'm sure I would have seen you around. You're different.'

Willie raised his head nervously. 'Am I?'

'Yes, I sensed that as soon as I saw you. There's someone who's a bit of a loner, I thought, an independent sort of a soul like myself, perhaps.' Willie glanced quickly at him. He felt quite tongue-tied. 'You're living with Mr Oakley, aren't you?' He nodded. 'He's a bit of a recluse, I believe.'

'Wot?' said Willie.

'A recluse. You know, keeps himself to himself.'

'Oh.'

'I say,' said Zach suddenly. 'We'll be at school together, won't we?'

He shrugged his shoulders again. 'I dunno.' He felt somewhat bewildered. He couldn't understand this exuberant friendliness in a boy he'd only had a glimpse of twice. It was all too fast for him to take in.

'I expect you think I'm a bit forward,' remarked Zach.

'Wot?'

'Forward. You know. But you see my parents work in the theatre and I'm so used to moving from town to town that I can't afford to waste time. As soon as I see someone I like, I talk to them.'

Willie almost dropped the clod of earth he was holding. No one had ever said that they liked him. He'd always accepted that no one did. Even his Mum said she only liked him when he was quiet and still. For her to like him he had to make himself invisible. He hurriedly put the earth on to the shelter.

Transformations

7 Transforming text

▶ Starting at the second dotted line, re-write the previous extract from *Goodnight Mister Tom* as a playscript. One way of writing the opening of the scene is shown below, but you will have to include the stage directions for what will be seen on stage. These will appear before any speech.

Write stage directions here (e.g. where the scene is set; who is already on stage at the start of the scene; who arrives on the scene now). Use 'Enter...' for the entry of new characters on stage as the scene progresses.		
ZACH	*Confident and happy*	Hello! (*Shaking hands with WILLIE*)
WILLIE	*Embarrassed at being covered in mud*	Sorry!
ZACH	*Not at all upset*	You're William Beech, aren't you? (*WILLIE nods*) Pleased to meet you. I'm Zacharias Wrench.

▶ In pairs or small groups, act out this scene in role, trying to use body language to express feelings. Then discuss how far this helps you understand each character's feelings and behaviour.

▶ Compare your new version with the original. Do you think you get a different impression of character or setting or anything else? How and why? Is it better or worse, or just different?

ADVICE

▲ You need to concentrate on what the characters say, and keep all the speech in at this stage.

▲ You need to set the scene. This means describing the set for the play at the start (i.e. so that stage designer would know what an audience will see on the stage at this point). The parts *before* the second dotted line will be needed for this.

▲ Your most important task is to give hints to performers about how they should say and act their part. This will include:
  • body language (e.g. looking away from someone, perhaps indicating shyness)
  • tone of voice (e.g. surprised/quiet).

The extracts for the following two activities are taken from the time when Willie returns for a visit to his mother in London. By this time he has got used to being evacuated and to staying at Mister Tom's house.

8 Transforming character

▶ Re-write the following two descriptions of their meeting at the railway station, turning Mrs Beech into the kind of mother Willie would really like to have.

> He studied her face. She was very pale, almost yellow in colour and her lips were so blue that it seemed as if every ounce of blood had been drained from them. The lines by her thin mouth curved downwards.
>
> ....
>
> They stood silently and awkwardly as the large noisy station roared around them. Willie felt his heart sinking and the spark of hope that he had held was fast dissolving, but then he remembered. Mister Tom had said that they would feel awkward at first and that it would take time to get used to each other.

9 Transforming place

▶ Re-write the following two descriptions, turning the cupboard under the stairs into Willie's own bedroom – the bedroom of his dreams.

> He woke up with a jerk, shivering with the cold. He began to stretch his cramped legs but they hurt. Opening his eyes he looked around in the darkness. He knew immediately where he was. He had been locked under the stairs. He peered through the crack at the side of the small door. It was pitch black. His mother must have gone to bed. He shivered. His boots were gone, so were his jersey and shorts.
>
> ....
>
> He took hold of the thin piece of material that lay under his body and wrapped it round himself.

Self-assessment

10 Judging your own performance

▶ From the list below:
  a select three points on which you feel you have made the most progress.
  b select one point on which you most need to improve.
  I can identify adjectives.
  I know if the connotation of a word is positive or negative.
  I understand why writers may choose to use non-standard English.
  I can write an extract from a novel in playscript form effectively.
  I can read between the lines, e.g. understand what descriptions of body language suggest.
  I can effectively transform a character presented negatively into a character presented positively.
  I can effectively transform a place presented negatively into a place presented positively.

11 Improving your skills in English

▶ Select one or two skills you need to concentrate on to improve your skills in reading. (The descriptions of levels are a guide, not a rulebook.)

	Reading skill	From	To
1	Show understanding of character	Level 3	Level 4
2	Begin to read between the lines	Level 3	Level 4
3	Select evidence to support ideas about a character	Level 4	Level 5
4	Read between the lines	Level 4	Level 5
5	Select words that demonstrate authors' techniques	Level 5	Level 6
6	Comment on effect of authors' techniques	Level 5	Level 6
7	Back up opinions on text with comment on theme, structure and language	Level 6	Level 7
8	Develop personal judgements based on sound evidence	Level 6	Level 7
9	Evaluate how authors achieve their effects	Level 7	Above Level 7
10	Appreciate and comment on a range of texts	Level 7	Above Level 7

4 Reading and writing non-fiction

The Centre for Alternative Technology

Your move

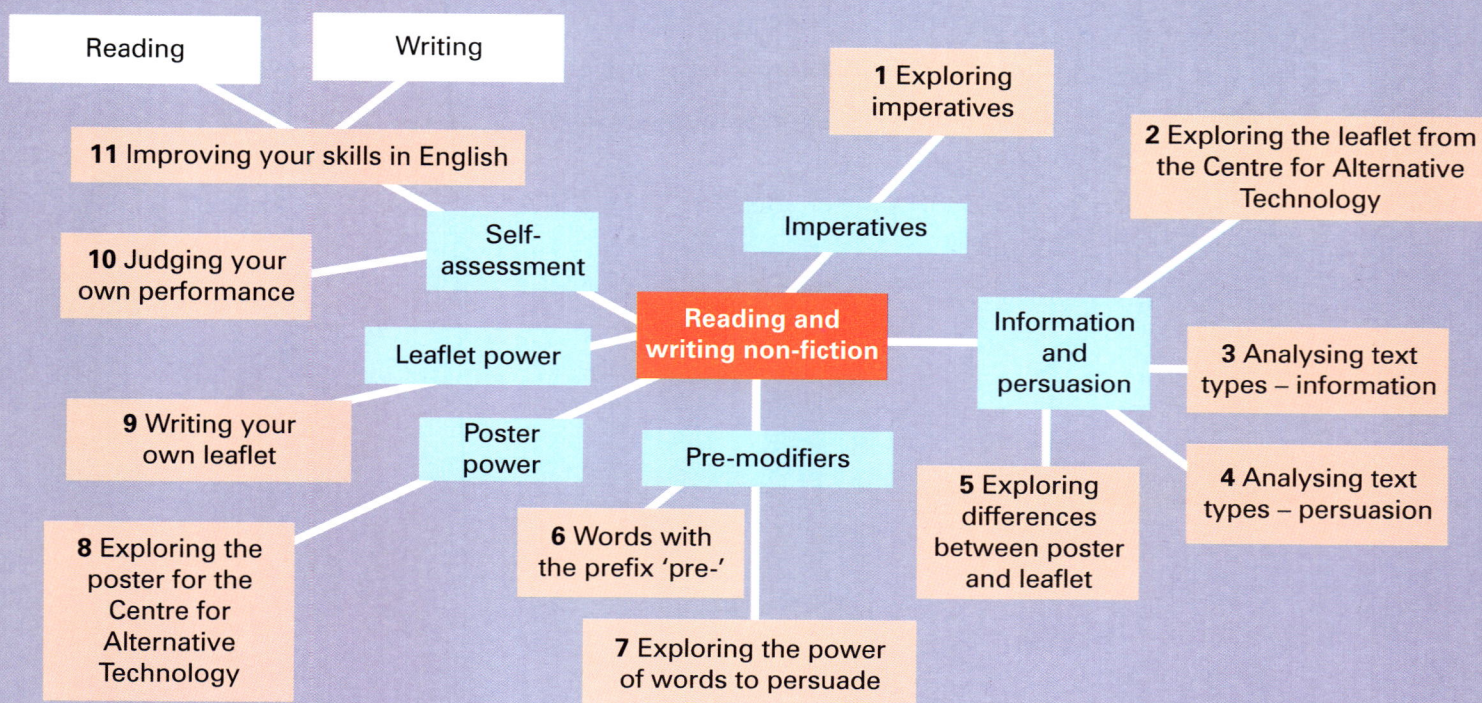

Reading

Writing

11 Improving your skills in English

10 Judging your own performance

Self-assessment

Leaflet power

9 Writing your own leaflet

Poster power

8 Exploring the poster for the Centre for Alternative Technology

6 Words with the prefix 'pre-'

Pre-modifiers

7 Exploring the power of words to persuade

Reading and writing non-fiction

Imperatives

1 Exploring imperatives

2 Exploring the leaflet from the Centre for Alternative Technology

Information and persuasion

3 Analysing text types – information

4 Analysing text types – persuasion

5 Exploring differences between poster and leaflet

Imperatives

To explore the texts in this unit effectively, you need to remember about imperatives. The *imperative* of a verb is used for giving orders, advice and instructions in a particularly direct way. When a verb is in the imperative, it is in its base form. The easiest way to check this is to start from the infinitive form, and leave out the word 'to'. Therefore, the infinitive forms, 'to go', 'to have', 'to see', 'to sit', 'to take' become:

● Go (at once)!
● Have (a try)!
● See (this film)!
● Sit (down)!
● Take (an aspirin)!

Imperatives are sometimes called 'bossy' words and at one time were referred to as commands.

1 Exploring imperatives

▶ How many of the examples of imperatives on the right do you think are 'bossy' words or commands? Be ready to justify your decision to other groups.
▶ In discussing your decisions, you may need to explore the tone of voice you might use in each case.

Reason for using imperative	Example
Commanding	Sit down!
Inviting	Have a drink.
Warning	Mind your head!
Pleading	Help me!
Suggesting	Let's walk.
Advising	Take an aspirin.
Instructing	Turn left.
Permitting	Help yourself.
Requesting	Open the window, please.
Thinking	Let me see.
Expressing good wishes	Enjoy your meal!
Expressing bad wishes	Go to hell!

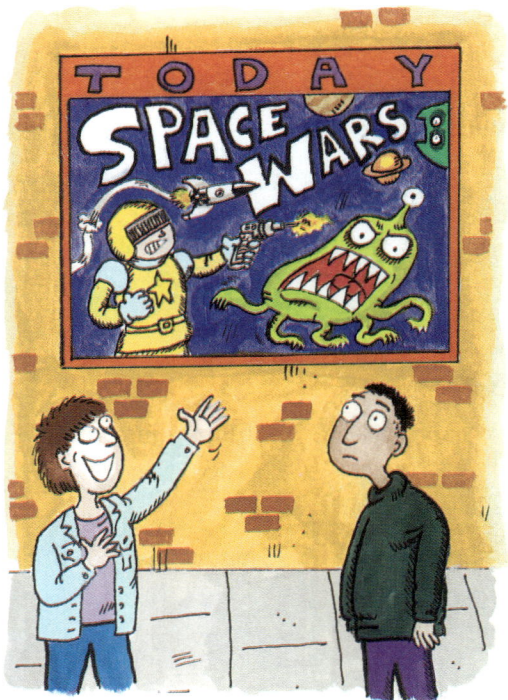

'See this film!'

'Sit down!'

'Take an asprin.'

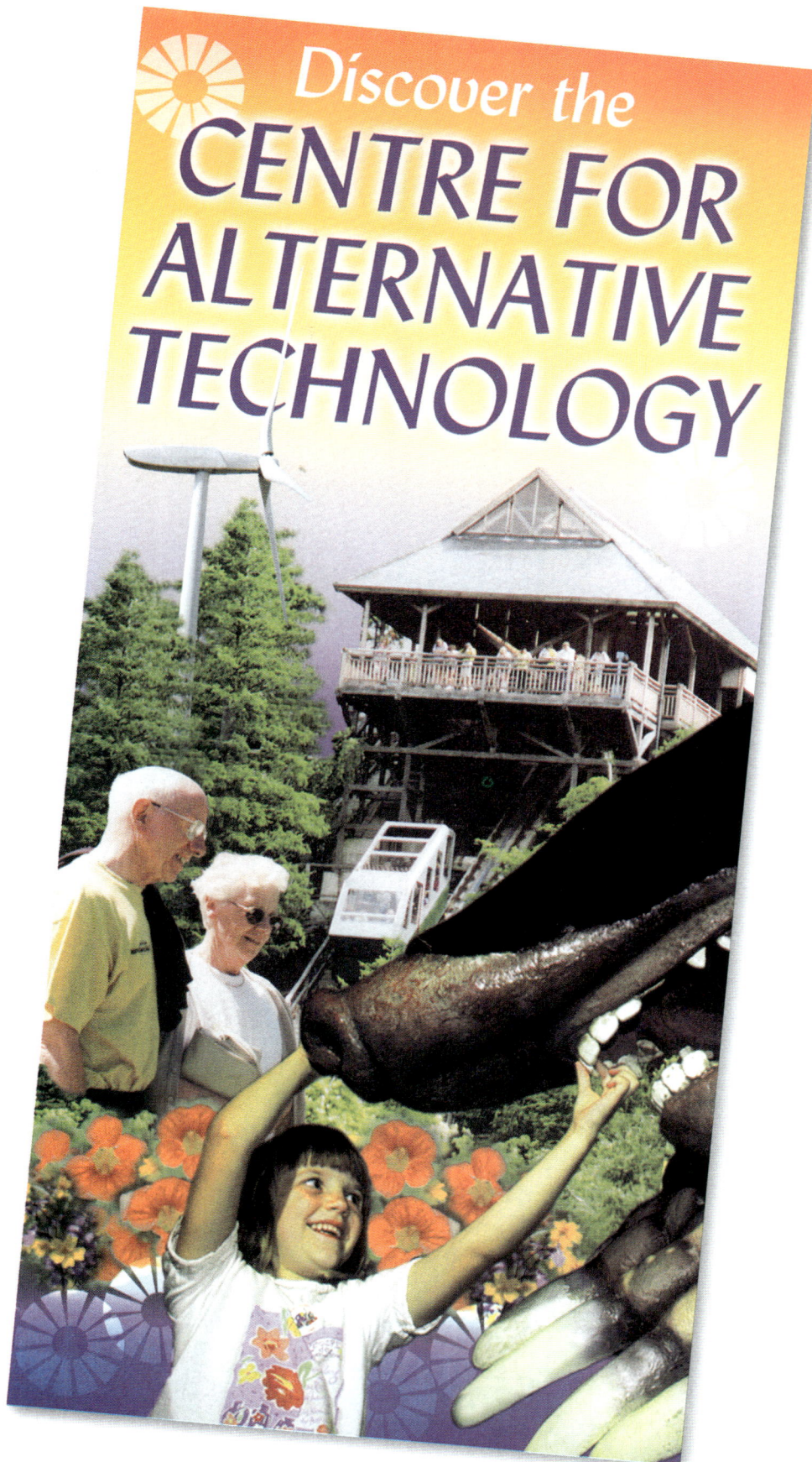

Discover the

CENTRE FOR ALTERNATIVE TECHNOLOGY

For Grown-ups

- ✔ Ride the water powered cliff railway (Easter - October)
- ✔ Relax in the tranquil organic gardens
- ✔ Take a special guided tour 'Behind the Scenes' during the peak season
- ✔ Sample vegetarian meals and snacks in our Egon Ronay recommended restaurant
- ✔ Explore seven acres of hands-on displays
- ✔ Bring your own picnic and enjoy the beautiful scenery of Mid Wales
- ✔ Discover how to save energy, save money and lots more....
- ✔ Browse in the unique book and gift shop

For Kids!

- ✔ Join in the Festival of the Future kids' theatre & games (only during school holidays)
- ✔ Journey underground to meet Megan the Mole
- ✔ Meet the farmyard animals
- ✔ Lose yourself in our Transport Maze
- ✔ Swing into action on our adventure playground
- ✔ Make a splash at the wave machine **and lots more....**

Great Discounts!

- ✔ Generous family discount ticket (2 adults and up to 4 children)
- ✔ Reductions for senior citizens, students, claimants and groups of 15 or more
- ✔ 10% discount if you arrive by bus
- ✔ 50% discount for cyclists
- ✔ 50% discount on standard cycle hire from Machynlleth (subject to availability) 'phone Greenstiles on (01654) 703543
- ✔ Joint rail ticket includes admission to CAT at up to 50% discount - available from Central Trains as far as Aberystwyth, Pwllheli and Wolverhampton

Set in beautiful countryside near Machynlleth and easy to find:

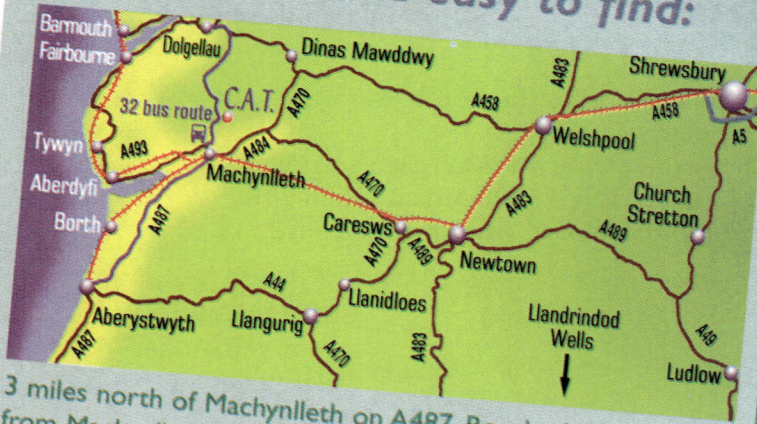

3 miles north of Machynlleth on A487. Regular bus services from Machynlleth railway station and other major towns.

Public Transport Information

The nearest bus stop is 300m distance, served by Arriva Cymru service 32 between Aberystwyth, Machynlleth and Dolgellau. Two hourly services, no service Sundays. The nearest railway station is Machynlleth, 6km, on the Aberystwyth - Shrewsbury and Cambrian Coaster routes. Two hourly service weekdays, no suitable service Sundays. Onward travel from Machynlleth by connecting bus. For further travel information, please contact the All Wales transport information service on 0870 608 2608 (opening 30 April 2000) National Rail Enquiries 08457 484950, Arriva Cymru 01248 750444.

A European funded marketing campaign

Education for sustainable living

Special rates and resources for educational parties. Call the Education Department for details (01654) 703743

Contact us at CAT,
Machynlleth, Powys,
SY20 9AZ
☎ (01654) 702400
or at www.cat.org.uk

Riverside camping and caravan site only 2 minutes walk from CAT
☎ 01654 702492

MILLENNIUM FESTIVAL

THE ATTRACTIONS OF SNOWDONIA

BWRDD CROESO CYMRU WALES TOURIST BOARD
ATYNIAD ARBENNIG STAR ATTRACTION

Assisted wheelchair access

Guide dogs only

Information and persuasion

2 Exploring the leaflet from the Centre for Alternative Technology

▶ Read the three pages of the leaflet from the Centre for Alternative Technology on pages 41 to 43.

▶ For each section of the leaflet, write down *what* each section includes, *why* you think each section is included and then write *Information* or *Persuasion* for each part, whichever fits best.

Discover the CENTRE FOR ALTERNATIVE TECHNOLOGY	For Grown-ups	Set in beautiful countryside near Machynlleth and easy to find:
	For Kids!	Public Transport Information
	Great Discounts!	Education for sustainable living

3 Analysing text types – information

▶ Some features of information texts are listed below. Give examples of any you can find in the leaflet, using a table like the one below.

Features of information texts	Examples in the leaflet
Headings/subheadings to arrange the information clearly	
Use of diagrams, etc. to make the information easy to understand	
Different size/colour of font to attract the reader's attention	
Information broken up into sections/boxes so the reader can find just the topic they want	
Use of the present tense	
Vocabulary of facts and figures, e.g. numbers, names of places/companies	
Far more nouns and verbs than adjectives and adverbs	

4 Analysing text types – persuasion

▶ Some features of persuasion texts are listed below. Give examples of any you can find in the leaflet, using a table like the one below.

Features of persuasion texts	Examples in the leaflet
Illustrations used to attract the reader	
Different size/colour of font to attract the reader's attention	
Use of imperatives	
Use of 'sentences' without verbs or full stops	
Use of 'purr' words to persuade	
Use of alliteration for effect (deliberate use of the same letter to start two or more words)	
Use of repetition for effect	

5 Exploring differences between the poster and the leaflet

▶ Study the poster for the Centre for Alternative Technology on the next page, and compare it with the leaflet on pages 41 to 43.
▶ What is similar, what is different and why?
▶ In what kind of place do you think you might see the poster, and in what kind of place do you think you might see the leaflet?
▶ What do you think might be printed on the back of the poster and on the back of the leaflet?
▶ How does where and how these are read affect the way they're designed?

Pre-modifiers

6 Words with the prefix 'pre-'

▶ Write a definition for five of these words, using 'before' or 'in advance' somewhere in the definition. Use a table like the one below.

Word	Definition using *before* or *in advance*
predate	
predict	
prefabricate	
prefix	
preheat	
prehistory	
prepackage	
prepay	
pre-release	
preset	
preshrunk	
prewash	

7 Exploring the power of words to persuade

▶ Notice how the nouns on the poster usually have pre-modifiers. For example, *water-powered cliff railway* limits the kind of railway being referred to, but also makes the railway seem far more special and interesting. On a poster like this, the pre-modifiers will be chosen to attract visitors.

▶ Find the pre-modifiers in the poster and list them in a table like the one below.

Pre-modifier	Pre-modifier	Noun
Water-powered	cliff	railway
		gardens
		events
		displays

▶ Choose one of the pre-modifiers you have found and say why you think the advertisers chose to use that word. How might that word make people more likely to go to the Centre?

WORDS

▲ **prefix** *noun* the beginning of a word that affects the whole word's meaning.
▲ **pre** *prefix* earlier than; in advance.

WORDS

▲ **modify** *transitive verb* make changes in; make different
▲ **pre-modifier** *adjective* a word that limits or changes the possible interpretations of the noun that follows it. For example, *bad dogs* limits **all dogs** to just **bad dogs**; *good dogs* limits **all dogs** to just **good dogs**. Both *good* and *bad* are called pre-modifiers here because they come before the noun *dog* and limit the kind of dogs the author is referring to. Of course, two different people might call the same dog good and bad.

Poster power

8 Exploring the poster from the Centre for Alternative Technology

▶ The poster is a collage of photos, logos, etc. combined to make a single picture.

▶ Why do you think the picture fills the whole poster and the poster only uses about 60 words in total?

▶ Find examples of the following techniques in the poster from the Centre for Alternative Technology. In your groups, try to give at least one reason why you think each technique has been used.

▶ Use a table like the one below.

Technique	Example	Why you think this technique has been used
Choosing pictures which show people enjoying themselves		
Choosing pictures which show a particular type of weather		
Using tripling (three examples together)		
Using people who may be recognised/may be well-known		
Using an exclamation		
Using a logo		
Giving contact details		

Leaflet power

9 Writing your own leaflet

▶ Write part of a leaflet for a place you know well which needs to attract visitors on a regular basis.

▶ Here are some suggestions, but you may come up with a good alternative of your own. Check with your teacher first:
  ● local leisure centre
  ● local market/shopping centre
  ● museum/gallery
  ● concert/sports/theatre venue (when an event is not in progress)
  ● outdoor pursuits centre.

▶ Your aim should be to write the text rather than design the whole leaflet, but you could write instructions to a designer making clear what you would like in terms of colour, pictures, logo, etc.

▶ Remember that such a leaflet should be informative and persuasive, and should make an appeal to different age groups. Try to include at least five of the following techniques:

Information	Persuasion
Use of clear diagram/map	Use of imperatives
Use of headings and sub-headings	Use of exclamation
Use of present tense	Use of pre-modifiers, making the place seem special
Use of helpful facts and figures	Use of repetition
Use of clearly presented contact details	Use of tripling (three examples together)

▶ When you have finished, name each technique you have used, and quote from your leaflet to show where you have used that technique.

▶ Write a separate explanation for each of the five techniques you have used that you are most proud of, explaining what effect you intend each example to have on a reader.

Self-assessment

10 Judging your own performance

▶ From the list below:
   a select three points on which you feel you have made the most progress.
   b select one point on which you most need to improve.

I know what imperatives are and can use them effectively in my own writing.
I can explain the differences between a poster and a leaflet.
I can recognise which parts of a leaflet or poster are designed to inform.
I can recognise which parts of a leaflet or poster are designed to persuade.
I can identify techniques used in leaflets and posters to inform, and use these techniques in my own writing.
I can identify techniques used in leaflets and posters to persuade, and use these techniques in my own writing.

11 Improving your skills in English

▶ Select one or two skills you need to concentrate on to improve your skills in reading. Then do the same for your writing skills. (The descriptions of levels are a guide, not a rulebook.)

Reading skill		From	To
1	Begin to use inference and deduction	Level 3	Level 4
2	Refer to the text when explaining views	Level 3	Level 4
3	Select essential points	Level 4	Level 5
4	Use inference and deduction where appropriate	Level 4	Level 5
5	Identify different layers of meaning	Level 5	Level 6
6	Comment on the significance and effect of details of the text	Level 5	Level 6
7	Show understanding of the ways in which meaning and information are conveyed	Level 6	Level 7
8	Select and synthesise a range of information from a variety of sources	Level 6	Level 7
9	Evaluate how authors achieve their effects through their use of linguistic, structural and presentational devices	Level 7	Above Level 7
10	Select and analyse information and ideas and comment on how these are conveyed in different texts	Level 7	Above Level 7

Writing skill		From	To
1	Ideas are organised appropriately for the purpose and the reader	Level 3	Level 4
2	Vocabulary choices are often adventurous and words are used for effect	Level 3	Level 4
3	A more formal style is used where appropriate	Level 4	Level 5
4	Vocabulary choices are imaginative and words are used precisely	Level 4	Level 5
5	The style and register is adapted to suit a leaflet and to suit the audience	Level 5	Level 6
6	A range of sentence structures and varied vocabulary are used to create effects	Level 5	Level 6
7	Writing is confident and shows an appropriate style for a leaflet and for the audience	Level 6	Level 7
8	Ideas are organised and coherent	Level 6	Level 7
9	Selection of specific features to convey particular effects	Level 7	Above Level 7
10	The writing is coherent, with use of vocabulary and grammar enabling fine distinctions to be made	Level 7	Above Level 7

5 Riddles, patterns and poems
My first is...

Your focus

The content of this unit is designed to:
- improve your skills in reading and writing poetry.

Your target

By the end of this unit you should be more able to:
- understand different types of pattern used in poems
- understand some of the techniques poets use
- use these techniques in your own poems
- read and perform poems effectively.

Your move

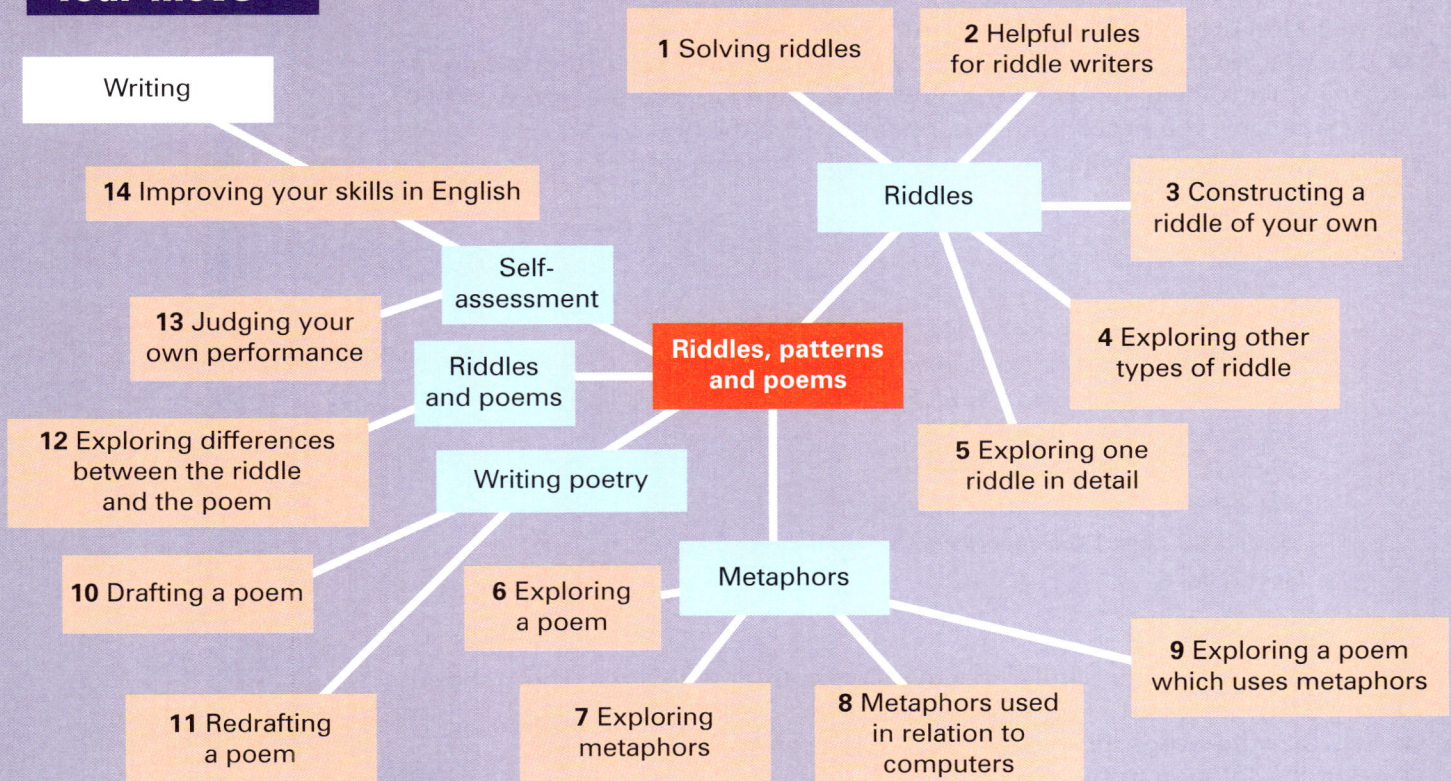

Writing

14 Improving your skills in English

13 Judging your own performance

12 Exploring differences between the riddle and the poem

10 Drafting a poem

11 Redrafting a poem

Self-assessment

Riddles and poems

Writing poetry

Riddles, patterns and poems

1 Solving riddles

2 Helpful rules for riddle writers

Riddles

3 Constructing a riddle of your own

4 Exploring other types of riddle

5 Exploring one riddle in detail

Metaphors

6 Exploring a poem

7 Exploring metaphors

8 Metaphors used in relation to computers

9 Exploring a poem which uses metaphors

Riddles

1 Solving riddles

▶ Read the following riddle.

Who Am I?

My first is in FOLLOW but not in LEAD,
My second's in RID but not in READ,
My third is the last letter in DEAL,
My fourth is the start of a midday meal,
The fifth is in HOME and also in POLE,
The last is in OWL but not in MOLE.
I stand by the lake more pale than brown,
With leaves and branches drooping down.
Who am I?

▶ What is the solution to the riddle? You must be able to track the thought process that led you to your solution. Be ready to explain to other groups how you came to your solution.
Note down:
- First we...
- Then we...
- Then we...
- We found the solution when we had these letters...
- The best strategies we used which could be used on similar riddles were...

▶ Decide what you will do differently next time when tackling this sort of riddle. What strategies you heard from other people were the best ones? See if you can use some of these strategies when solving the following riddle.

Riddle

My first is in fish but not in chip.
My second in teeth but not in lip.
My third's in potato but not in plum.
My fourth's in mouth and also in thumb.
My fifth is in pear but not in cherry.
My sixth is in bacon but not in berry.
My last is in chocolate but not in crumble.
Sometimes when I'm empty you'll hear me rumble.
John Foster

▶ How is the above riddle similar to and different from *Who Am I?* Think about:
- use of rhyming
- whether the words the author chooses have any connection with the solution to the riddle.

2 Helpful rules for riddle writers

▶ How could you give someone helpful advice on writing a riddle like those in Activity 1? Imagine someone has never seen or read a riddle before. What are the essential points?

▶ Write some helpful rules for riddle writers.

ADVICE

▲ You will need to give advice on:
  • the number of lines used
  • where to hide the letters
  • the length of each line
  • how to end your riddle
  • a suitable title.

▲ Start with a title such as 'How to write a riddle – helpful rules for riddle writers'.

▲ Keep the sentences short, clear and helpful.

▲ You may need to use words such as rhyme, riddle and solution.

▲ You may find it helpful to use imperatives such as:
  • Start
  • Use
  • Choose
  • Select
  • Make sure
  • Give
  • Don't.

3 Constructing a riddle of your own

▶ You will be following your own advice and writing a riddle. You will be spending some time on the subject you choose, so make sure it is one you have plenty to write about. Possibilities include:
  ● a person you know well
  ● a dog, a cat, or some other animal that you can describe in detail
  ● a television
  ● a computer.

ADVICE

▲ If you are choosing to write about a cat or dog, you will need to use the name of the animal rather than just have a three-line riddle (which is too easy to solve when it is of this type).

▲ You will have to give enough information to allow the reader to guess the type of animal as well as work out its name.

▲ An alternative would be to use a word such as 'kitten', which refers to one particular type of cat.

▶ Follow your own helpful rules for riddle writers and construct your own riddle.

ADVICE

▲ In some riddles there is some sort of connection between the two key words in each line. For example, FOLLOW obviously matches LEAD in the first line of *Who Am I?*. It could make your riddle sound more thoughtful and planned if you try to do the same, at least for some of the lines.

▲ The second riddle is even more ambitious, with words selected to link with the solution as well as to rhyme in pairs of lines. Don't expect it to be easy if you try this in your own riddle.

▲ The best advice would be to start with any words that provide a solution and then see if you can improve on your choice in some way – either by trying to use rhyme or by linking the words.

▲ You could also add one or two lines *after* you have used one line for each letter, as in *Who Am I?*. This can give different kinds of clues about the solution to the riddle.

4 Exploring other types of riddle

▶ There is another type of riddle which works in a different way.
▶ Work out a possible solution for each of the next two riddles, and be prepared to explain how you came to your decision.

Riddle 1

The more you hold him
The thinner he grows,
The wetter he gets
The brighter he glows.

The lither and leaner
The slimmer his shape,
The more likely he is
To want to escape.

The more he escapes
The more he grows leaner
Each time you touch him
You feel that much cleaner.

Riddle 2

I know a man — he lives in the wall,
He does his work by running about,
He runs up the ceiling — and there's light!
He runs into a box — and there is music!
He leaps across the street and our phone rings.
He runs about so much he gets quite hot.
Don't touch him or he'll kick you.

▶ Once again, you must be able to track the thought process that led you to your solution. You will have to explain to other groups how you came to your solution.
▶ What does 'he'll kick you' refer to? Why does the writer use the word 'kick'?
▶ How are these riddles different from *Who Am I?*?

5 Exploring one riddle in detail

▶ Read the following riddle and work out who or what you think the writer might be referring to.

> I am
> word-cruncher
> wilful, square brain,
> a mind of my own;
> I am words without end,
> though silent as stone.
> My head is a jumble
> of poems not yet done;
> a mumble of stories,
> of number, of song.
> I'm a dream-hoarder —
> snatch my words,
> catch if you can!
> Snatch them and mix them,
> make them your own.
>
> Judith Nicholls

▶ In your group, come up with ideas for what the 'word-cruncher' might be.

ADVICE

It may help you to think about:
▲ what words are repeated.
▲ why this person or thing might be silent.
▲ what the square brain might refer to.

▶ Once you know the author's idea, work out in more detail what is being compared to what. Write down what you think is the connection between the word in the poem and the solution to the riddle, using a table like the one below.

Quotation from riddle	What it refers to	Connection
word-cruncher		
square brain		

▶ How would you explain 'words without end'?
▶ How would you explain 'I'm a dream-hoarder'?
▶ What do you think is meant by the last two lines?
▶ Report your findings back to the other groups.

Metaphors

6 Exploring a poem

▶ In all types of speech and writing, metaphors such as 'word-cruncher' and 'square brain' are used. Sometimes there is a link between the metaphors.

▶ What connection can you find between any of the metaphors in the following poem? Read the whole poem first, and work out what you think is happening here.

The Errand

'On you go now! Run, son, like the devil
And tell your mother to try
To find me a bubble for the spirit level
And a new knot for this tie.'

But still he was glad, I know, when I stood my ground,
Putting it up to him
With a smile that trumped his smile and his fool's errand,
Waiting for the next move in the game.

Seamus Heaney

▶ Who are the three people involved here?

▶ Who is 'speaking' the poem? How old is this person, do you think?

▶ In your group, come to an agreement about what is going on here.

▶ Find a word that is repeated, and work out why you think it is repeated.

▶ What can you tell about the relationship between the characters?

▶ What is the connection between some of the metaphors?

7 Exploring metaphors

▶ Metaphors are part of everyday conversation, but sometimes they are so common that we forget they started as metaphors.

▶ Match up the words in the left-hand column with words from the box below to make a common metaphor.

▶ Using a table like the one here, note down what you think connects the two in a common expression or saying. One example has been completed for you.

bell
Italy
school
chair
moon
stairs
clock/watch
plane
story
hurricane
plane
teeth

ITALY
Rome

Word	Common saying	What connects the two
Arm	Arm of a chair	One on each side of the main part of the human body/chair
Eye		
Face		
Foot		
Hand		
Head		
Leg		
Nose		
Skin		
(Twist in the) tail		
Toe		
Tongue		
Wing		

8 Metaphors used in relation to computers

▶ When we want a new word for a new object, we often look for similarities with things that already have names. Of course, these are all metaphors, but we don't think of them as metaphors because the freshness of the original comparison is lost. Many new words connected with computers are also metaphors. Fill in a table like the one below as fully as you can.

▶ In the column headed 'X', note down what the word usually refers to outside the world of computers.

▶ In the column headed 'Y', note down what the word has come to mean when applied to the world of computers.

▶ In the column headed 'Link/effect', try to explain the connection between X and Y – why has this word been used for this new idea?

▶ In the empty box at the bottom of the left-hand column, add any other words you can think of which have been taken from other meanings and applied in a new way to computers. Then try to fill in the X, Y and Link/effect boxes for your chosen word(s).

Metaphor	X	Y	Link/effect
Browse			
Crash			
Hack			
Menu			
Net			
Scroll			
Surf			

9 Exploring a poem which uses metaphors

▶ Read the poem on the right, *Acrobats*.

▶ In your group, decide what the poem is about. Select three details that you think will persuade the other groups that your conclusion is the best one.

▶ You won't find the word 'scurtle' (line 5) in a dictionary. What words does it remind you of? What do you think it means? How can you tell?

▶ What's the connection between acrobats and clowns? Why are the humans described as clowns, do you think?

▶ Mike Jenkins uses half-rhyme in much of the poem, e.g. stile/pole; bounds/clowns. Work out in your group why you think this might be.

▶ Select the one detail from the poem that you find the most interesting. Prepare to explain your choice to the rest of the class.

Acrobats

October's under soil and in the air:
have you heard them say it clear?
It's a clatter of twigs snapping,
a free-fall of nuts cracking.

They scurtle along a sloping wire
fast as waves of sound,
eyes full of harvest fires
whose ashes are spread around.

Look at those humble acrobats
those much-maligned tree-rats,
lighter than leaves on thinnest branch
leaping from the frailest launch.

Below they're nervy in garden's ring,
on two legs losing their furry wings;
acorns rolled between their claws
buried for times when they'll be poor.

Two ladders, the fence and the stile,
chasing each other, knowing no bounds,
the oak's trunk is a steady pole:
bring on the humans, the clowns.

Mike Jenkins

Writing poetry

10 Drafting a poem

▶ You are now going to return to the subject you chose for your riddle and create a poem of your own on the same topic.

▶ Some of you may be quite used to writing your own poems, others less so. The guidance that follows is intended to help you create a good poem, but if you have plenty of ideas of your own you may be able to go ahead independently.

▶ Think back to Judith Nicholls's riddle about the word-cruncher. That riddle suggested that we as writers have to unlock the dreams, ideas and possibilities that all of us hold in our heads.

I'm a dream-hoarder —
snatch my words,
catch if you can!
Snatch them and mix them,
make them your own.

▶ That is the challenge of this activity – to 'mix' words in such a way that your thoughts are communicated to other people and the dream is no longer hoarded.

▶ In the extract below, Mike Jenkins describes some of the background to his writing *Acrobats*. This may give you some ideas for your own poem.

The idea for this poem came from observing a couple of grey squirrels who often visit our garden. Their acrobatics impressed me greatly, as they leapt from fence to tree and moved rapidly along the telephone wires. They seemed very different when they were in the tree than on the ground, where they were more wary.

I was particularly amazed one day to hear the sound of one squirrel. It was similar to the magpie with quite a cackling, mocking tone.

Compared to them, I do see humans as clowns in the circus of the natural world. We are awkward creatures, comical not graceful in our movements for the most part and the squirrel serves to highlight this.

A good way to follow up the poem would be to look at various animals and depict their many talents. You don't need to go to a circus to admire these. One vision of a barn owl hunting at night across moors will stay in my imagination longer than any 'tricks'. Think of the flamingo, a stilt-walker with a purpose. Or, what better clowns than penguins? You can see where Charlie Chaplin got his walk from!

The use of half-rhymes in the poem wasn't deliberate. I tend to write very instinctively. The subject-matter determines the style. So, if the half-rhyme does suggest their quick changes of direction and hurried movements, then, hopefully, I've succeeded.

I also like to use 'made-up' words at times. The word 'scurtle' is a portmanteau word, that is to say a combination of 'scurry' and 'hurtle'. The writers Thomas Hardy and James Joyce are inspirations for this kind of adventurous word-craft.

When you've chosen one animal to describe, you might like to make up a word which fits its sound, colour or movement.

Squirrels are pests, but I like them a lot. Maybe that's why I'm a teacher!

ADVICE

Writing about animals is just one possibility, of course. Whatever subject you chose earlier, use the following suggestions and then see if they help you create your own poem:

▲ Write down the one thing which is most special about your chosen topic.

▲ Make a list of words which you associate with your chosen topic.

▲ Mike Jenkins compares his chosen topic with acrobats. If you were to compare your chosen topic with something/someone else, what comparison would help another person understand your chosen topic/your attitude to your chosen topic? (You may find you are using a metaphor.)

▲ Mike Jenkins contrasts the very different behaviour of his chosen topic in different places – on a wire, in a tree, in a garden. Choose words which will show how different your chosen topic can be in different situations.

▲ You do not need to use all these ideas, but they may help you get started.

▲ As you consider your poem, aim to:
• write between 10 and 20 lines
• avoid rhyming unless you are convinced it is needed
• experiment with deleting words to see if you can improve the sound of your poem when you are finishing your first draft (you will have to work out for each decision if cutting words makes the poem more effective or not).

▲ Possible structure:
• first stanza – the person/animal/object when asleep/silent
• second stanza – the person/animal/object when alert/active/noisy.

WORDS

▲ **portmanteau** *noun* large bag or case for a traveller's belongings that opens into two equal parts.

11 Redrafting a poem

▶ Now you have completed a first draft, read the following poem to see if it gives you ideas for how to improve it for a second draft.

Tutorial

I know: the words came flooding into your head,
and you just wrote them down... Now look again;
work out what you really wanted to say,
and how you failed to say it. Then you can.

And yes, some of it works. So concentrate
on what doesn't. And when *that* takes off,
go back to what you thought were the good bits
and craft them better. Good's not good enough.

Play with the line. Turn it around, and see
what happens. Try taking a stress away;
change tense, loosen the rhythm. Shake the words up
like patterns in a kaleidoscope. Just play.

Climb into someone else's story,
think in his voice, bring him alive, move on
to the next. Become a vent act, a shape-changer.
Why settle for just you? Be everyone.

Open up: look and listen so hard,
it hurts. Taste the frost on the air,
the blood on your tongue. Half-alive is too dull
for words; will make no mark on blank paper.

Argue back. Tell me I'm wrong. I've been doing
the same tricks for years: make me learn,
surprise me. Take a word for a walk
down a new road where I have never been.

Take your gift and polish it; make it shine
bright enough for praise, too bright for jealousy.
The best work any artist can leave
is a pupil who outshines him. Go beyond me.

Sheenagh Pugh

▶ Write a final draft of your poem, taking into account some of the advice offered by Sheenagh Pugh in her poem.
▶ Prepare a reading for the whole class to hear. Make notes for yourself on your copy reminding yourself how to read each part of the poem to make it come alive for others in the class.

Riddles and poems

12 Exploring differences between the riddle and the poem

▶ Write two or three paragraphs on the differences between your riddle from Activity 3 and your poem on the same subject. You might like to comment on:

- how many of the words help to create a real idea of the person, animal or object
- which one has more variety in rhythm
- which one has the more interesting choice of words/is more exciting to read
- how far you have to read and understand every word in each
- which of the two you prefer and why.

▶ Start with the smaller details, such as your choice of words in each, and gradually move on to the larger details, such as which one you prefer overall.

ADVICE

Possible connectives to use when comparing the riddle and poem:

- ▲ but
- ▲ compared with
- ▲ however
- ▲ in contrast
- ▲ instead of
- ▲ is different from
- ▲ on the contrary
- ▲ on the other hand
- ▲ unlike
- ▲ whereas
- ▲ yet the other

▶ Now sum up the main differences using four or five bullet points.

Self-assessment

13 Judging your own performance

▶ From the list below:

   a select three points on which you feel you have made the most progress.

   b select one point on which you most need to improve.

I can write clear rules for one type of riddle.

I can write a riddle following my own rules.

I understand the link between a literal meaning and a metaphor, e.g. surf a wave (literal meaning), surf the net (metaphorical meaning). (Add your own example.)

I can write a poem choosing my words carefully.

I can write a poem using metaphors.

I can re-draft a poem and make significant improvements.

I can comment on significant differences between my riddle and my poem on the same subject.

I know the difference between a riddle and a poem. (Explain the difference in your own way.)

I have learnt some ways to improve my poetry writing by following the advice of others.

14 Improving your skills in English

▶ Select one or two skills you need to concentrate on to improve your skills in writing. (The descriptions of levels are a guide, not a rulebook.)

	Writing skill	From	To
1	Vocabulary choices are adventurous and words are used for effect	Level 3	Level 4
2	Vocabulary choices are imaginative and words are used precisely	Level 4	Level 5
3	Use a range of sentence structures and varied vocabulary to create effects	Level 5	Level 6
4	Grammatical features and vocabulary are accurately and effectively used	Level 6	Level 7
5	The use of vocabulary and grammar enables fine distinctions to be made	Level 7	Above Level 7

6 Discussion and discursive writing
Mobile?

Your focus

The content of this unit is designed to:
- improve your skills in speaking and writing persuasively.

Your target

By the end of this unit you should be more able to:
- take an active part in a debate and have your ideas listened to
- write in a way that is likely to persuade
- explain your point of view clearly and effectively.

Your move

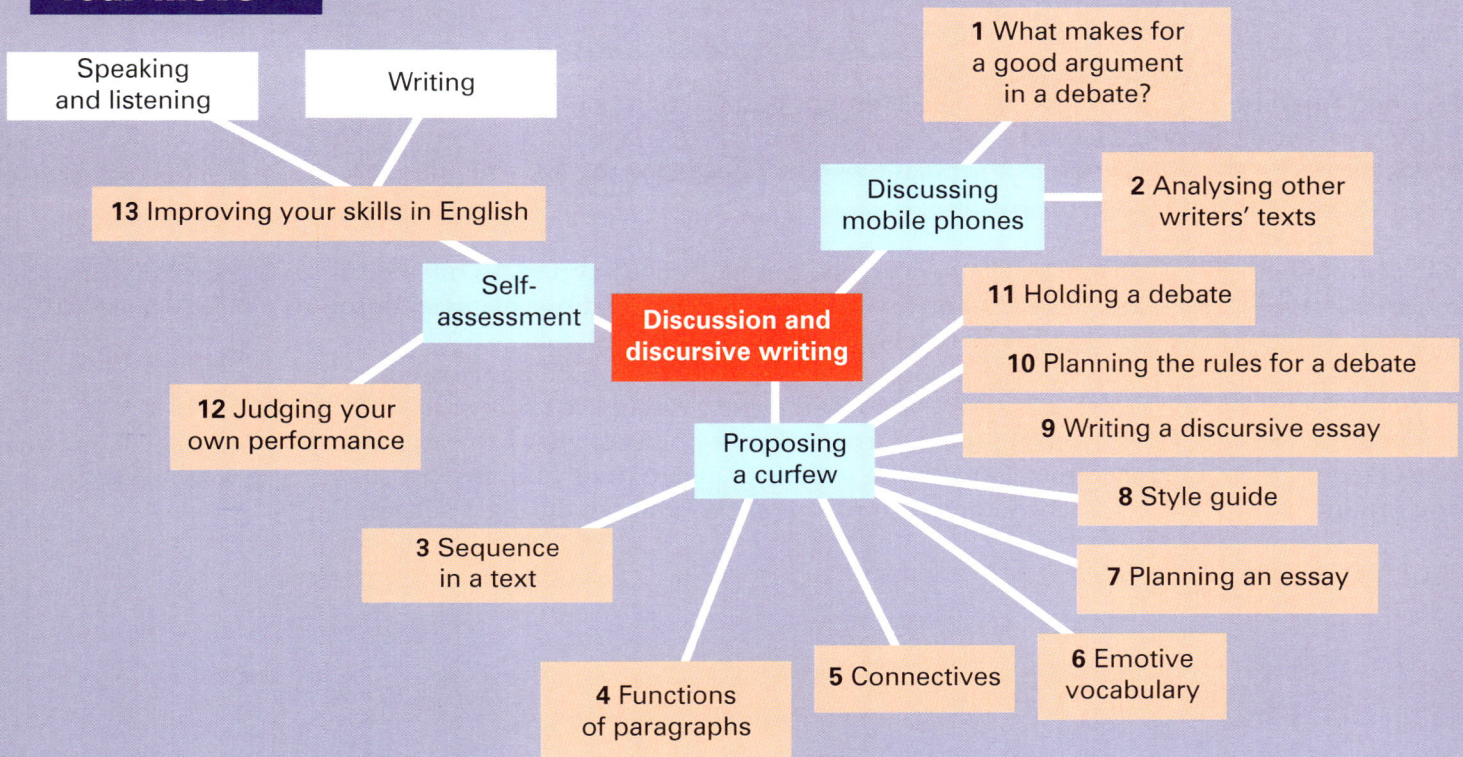

Speaking and listening

Writing

13 Improving your skills in English

Self-assessment

12 Judging your own performance

3 Sequence in a text

Discussion and discursive writing

Proposing a curfew

4 Functions of paragraphs

5 Connectives

6 Emotive vocabulary

1 What makes for a good argument in a debate?

Discussing mobile phones

2 Analysing other writers' texts

11 Holding a debate

10 Planning the rules for a debate

9 Writing a discursive essay

8 Style guide

7 Planning an essay

Discussing mobile phones

1 **What makes for a good argument in a debate?**

▶ In groups, rank the following in order from 1 to 6, with the best strategy as number 1.

The best way to present an argument

a Disagreeing with the argument of a person, not finding fault with the person.
b Repeating your argument until other people agree with you.
c Listening to the other point of view carefully before replying.
d Organising the order of your thoughts before speaking.
e Saying what you feel strongest about first.
f Trying to put down the person you disagree with.

▶ When you have decided on the order as a group, start following your own advice and prepare to argue to the rest of the class why your order is the best.
▶ If you want to convince someone that your argument is a good one, how do you think you will succeed? (You must rely on words alone, of course.)
▶ In the same groups, rank the following in order from 1 to 4, with the best strategy as number 1.

The best way to prove your point

a Backing up your argument with examples from other people's experience.
b Backing up your argument with examples from your own experience.
c Backing up your argument with statements from official organisations.
d Backing up your argument with statistics.

▶ When you have decided on the order as a group, prepare to argue to the rest of the class why your order is the best.
▶ Are there any other ways you can persuade people effectively? (Again, you must rely on words alone, in speech or writing.)

If everyone follows the rules in a debate, everyone can have their say and no one needs to feel put down. The ideal is that no one leaves the room (or debating chamber) upset after the debate because they didn't have a chance to have their say.

In a debate in class, some people will probably be *for* the motion being debated, other people will be *against* the motion. When you *write* a discursive essay, you present both sides of the argument yourself. The different points of view can easily be presented in separate paragraphs. Usually you will have time to draft your answer, so you can include all those points you didn't think up quickly enough during a debate.

WORDS

▲ **argument** *noun* **1** the act or process of argument; debate. **2** a coherent series of reasons offered.

WORDS

▲ **motion** *noun* a proposal for formal discussion at a meeting.

2 Analysing other writers' texts

▶ Read the following discursive essay about mobile phones in school.

Over the last few years, mobile phones have become common in schools and 11- and 12-year-olds are no exception. Some schools ban all mobile phones from the whole school, some schools just insist they should be turned off in the classroom. In this essay I will discuss the issues and make clear what my conclusion is.

Those who argue against the use of mobile phones in school altogether say that mobile phones disrupt school life. Even if phones are meant to be switched off in the classroom, it's inevitable that someone will forget or even deliberately leave theirs on. It is very irritating if you are involved in a science experiment or in the middle of a play reading and the whole atmosphere is destroyed by someone's phone ringing. Others argue against mobile phones by saying there is a health risk of radiation, particularly to young people, and that for this reason alone they should be banned.

However, there are also people who argue that mobile phones are a positive benefit in schools. In many jobs oral skills are essential, and pupils who are brought up used to communicating regularly in speech will develop these skills far more than those who don't use mobile phones. In addition, mobile phones make it much easier for schools to be adaptable. If someone is needed for a rehearsal or for a sports team at the last minute, they can phone home quickly and easily to make the necessary arrangements.

In my opinion there may be health risks, but we don't know enough about these yet, and until there is more proof we should go on using them. Young people enjoy communicating with their friends using mobile phones, and these phones are here to stay anyway – they can't be 'uninvented'. So I think schools should welcome them as a way of promoting speaking and listening skills and letting pupils use the latest technologies. If their phone rings during a lesson it should be confiscated for at least 24 hours. This would soon persuade those who disrupt lessons accidentally or deliberately to change their behaviour.

ADVICE

▲ Different types of text use different types of words.

▲ The words 'mobile phone' might be found in an advertisement, a bill, a discursive piece like the one here, or a report in a science journal on the safety of mobile phones. So the words 'mobile phone' are not helpful in showing what is special about discursive texts.

▲ The words 'my conclusion' are more helpful. These words suggest that the piece of writing will come to a decision of some kind: discursive essays and reviews are texts which come to some kind of decision.

▶ Identify the words which help to tell you this is piece of discursive writing.

▶ A good strategy for improving your writing is to see how other writers use language, and copy their good ideas. Some parts of the writing on mobile phones could be used in a discursive piece of writing on another topic. Later in this unit you will be drafting your own piece of discursive writing. What parts of the mobile phone text do you think you could use?

▶ Write down five parts of sentences/techniques from this text which you think could be most useful in *your own* discursive writing about a *different* topic.

▶ Suggest a title for each paragraph which sums up what the author is doing in that paragraph.

Proposing a curfew

Read extracts **A** to **I** below, which have been taken from one source and are not in the correct sequence.

A Another argument against the proposal is that it would prevent perfectly safe activities. A young person on a farm may well be doing jobs around the farm early in the morning, and the policy is not appropriate in this case. In many areas there will be young people doing newspaper or milk rounds during the time of the curfew. Those who argue this way say it is ridiculous to restrict young people so drastically.

B Crime is one of the biggest problems in our society, making some people unwilling to leave their homes after dark. As part of an attempt to cut down on crime, it has been suggested that any child below the age of 11 should be banned from being outside their home after 10 p.m. every evening, until 6 a.m. the next morning, unless accompanied by a parent or guardian, or by an adult approved by the parent or guardian.

C On the other hand, organisations such as Liberty argue against curfews. They say this policy is an abuse of personal choice and freedom. Why shouldn't young people be allowed to walk freely when they want?

D The police also support this suggestion as a way of reducing crime. If there are fewer young people around, those who are around and are causing problems are far more easily noticed and caught.

E In addition, some people say the policy just will not work. There simply aren't enough police men and women available to go round the streets and catch those breaking the curfew. In any case, how can they tell the exact age of a person just by looking?

F Should there be a curfew on all children below the age of 11 after 10 p.m.?

G Apart from these arguments in favour, there is also evidence to support the policy. A curfew like this has been tried in some parts of the USA, where crime has been reduced by 80 per cent. Those who have seen how successful it is think it should be extended to all towns and cities in the USA.

H In conclusion, if crime can be reduced as dramatically as in the USA, it must be worth considering the policy. However, it is clearly not suited to every locality, and only local people, not central government, can decide if it should apply in their area. To allow for different conditions in different areas, the local council should be allowed to operate the system it thinks is best in its area.

I One argument for this suggestion is that young people are very likely to be involved in crimes involving damage to parked cars, vandalism of telephone boxes and vandalism in residential areas. Most of this activity takes place at night, and stopping young people being out at this time is a simple and easy way to reduce crime.

3 Sequence in a text

▶ Work out the sequence you think is most logical for extracts **A** to **I**.
▶ Write down the words that you have used to help you make your decisions.

4 Functions of paragraphs

▶ Give labels for each paragraph **A** to **I** of the new text, saying what you think that part of the text is doing – its function in the overall discursive essay.

5 Connectives

▶ Each text type tends to have its own linking words or connectives. Common linking words are 'and', 'but', 'if', 'or', 'because'.
▶ Identify and write down linking words or connectives which are used in extracts **A** to **I** and which you might be able to use in a discursive text of your own.

6 Emotive vocabulary

▶ Look back at the 'purr' and 'snarl' words about Mister Tom's dog in Unit 3 (pages 31 and 32). Identify and write down any examples of emotive vocabulary you can find in the following two sentences.

> Those who argue this way say it is ridiculous to restrict young people so drastically.

> In conclusion, if crime can be reduced as dramatically as in the USA, it must be worth considering the policy.

WORDS

▲ **emotive** *adjective* arousing or appealing to emotion, especially as opposed to reason.

ADVICE

▲ Look for words that have a strong effect, i.e. single words designed to influence your opinion for or against the proposal and which you might use in a discursive text of your own.

7 Planning an essay

▶ You are going to write an essay with the title 'Should there be a curfew from 10 p.m. to 6 a.m. on all children below the age of 11?'

▶ Plan your essay by giving a title to each paragraph (in the same way you gave a title to each paragraph in the mobile phones text on page 65). Be prepared to justify your decision to the rest of the group and to other groups.

▶ Write one paragraph for the middle section of your essay, using this order:
  ● a statement of what some people think
  ● some evidence to back it up
  ● your opinion on the statement.

▶ Be prepared to read it to your group and other groups, explaining what you have done and why.

8 Style guide

▶ Some examples of what other pupils have written when tackling this unit are given below. Decide in each case whether:
  ● it is suitable in style for a discursive essay
  ● the argument is clearly stated
  ● there is a better way of saying it.

▶ Organise your ideas in a table like the one below.

Example	Suitable for a discursive essay or not?	Is the argument clearly stated? Can you suggest a better way of saying it?
My parents think you shouldn't be allowed out after 10 p.m.: you need rules to learn to respect people and you need a good night's sleep in order to learn next day		
As part of an attempt to have not as much crime, some people think there should be a curfew		
My conclusion is that people should be made aware about the risks before letting their child out after 10 p.m.		
These crimes usually take place at night, so to stop these crimes we don't let children out after 10 p.m.		
I, as a pupil, think it unfair that we should be restricted to times against our own free will		
If crime can be put down as much as it has in the USA, it must be worth considering the curfew		

9 Writing a discursive essay

▶ You are now in a good position to write a discursive essay based on this topic. You can use some of the ideas provided, but include some extra material as well.

▶ Write a discursive essay on the suggestion that there should be a curfew for young people.

▶ Don't forget to use any of the words or parts of sentences you have selected from the discursive texts by other writers. However, do not copy whole sentences.

▶ Additional issues you might like to consider:
- What age group should have the curfew, if any?
- Could the times of the curfew be changed?
- Is there a better alternative?
- Is it true that young people cause so much of the problem of crime?

ADVICE

▲ Have a clear topic for each paragraph, e.g. Introduction, For, Against, Conclusion. But do not label the paragraphs – these are simply headings in your mind.

▲ Help the reader follow your line of thought, e.g. by using a clear opening sentence for each paragraph and by stating each view clearly.

▲ Think ahead to how your reader may react, and answer any points they might make.

▲ Use connectives such as 'however', 'on the other hand', 'nevertheless', 'but', and 'although'.

▲ Back up each point you make with examples, evidence, reasons and statistics.

▲ Name any sources you quote, especially more official ones.

▲ Come to a definite conclusion on the topic.

10 Planning the rules for a debate

▶ You will be having a debate on the issues you have been discussing in class.

▶ Many of the arguments that you have developed for your written piece can be used for the debate in class. However, you would not get very far in a debate if you started reading out your essay, or even reciting it from memory. Why do you think this is?

▶ Make a list of the five most important rules you can think of for making the debate interesting and successful.

▶ Decide as a class which five rules the whole class will adopt when conducting the debate.

ADVICE

Think about the following when devising your rules:

▲ You will need to hear each other's points of view clearly.

▲ You will need to make sure no one feels they are ignored or put down.

▲ You will need to make sure everyone has an opportunity to speak.

▲ It would be interesting to know if the debate has changed people's opinions.

▲ The debate will be of higher quality if people back up what they say with evidence, rather than just asserting that they are right.

11 Holding a debate

▶ Hold a debate on the motion 'There should be a curfew from 10 p.m. to 6 a.m. on all children below the age of 11.'

Self-assessment

12 Judging your own performance

▶ From the list below:

  a select three points on which you feel you have made the most progress.

  b select one point on which you most need to improve.

  I can present my point of view in a debate.

  I can argue against someone else's point of view in speech without being personal.

  I can present arguments for and against a point of view in an essay.

  I can organise my paragraphs in a clear and logical way, which the reader can follow.

  I can give evidence for a point of view from my own experience.

  I can give evidence for a point of view using the experience of other people.

▶ Write down one strategy you could adopt to help you improve on the area you have targeted for improvement. (Discuss this with your teacher if you need to.)

13 Improving your skills in English

▶ Select one or two skills you need to concentrate on to improve your skills in speaking and listening. Then do the same for your writing skills. (The descriptions of levels are a guide, not a rulebook.)

	Speaking and listening skill	From	To
1	Listen carefully, making contributions and asking questions that are responsive to others' ideas and views	Level 3	Level 4
2	Pay close attention to what others say and ask questions to develop ideas	Level 4	Level 5
3	Make contributions that take account of others' views	Level 4	Level 5
4	Take an active part in discussion, showing understanding of ideas and sensitivity to others	Level 5	Level 6
5	Make significant contributions, evaluating others' ideas	Level 6	Level 7
6	Vary when and how they participate	Level 6	Level 7
7	Make a range of contributions which show that they have listened perceptively	Level 7	Above Level 7
8	Show they are sensitive to the development of discussion	Level 7	Above Level 7

	Writing skill	From	To
1	The ideas in the essay are organised in a logical order	Level 3	Level 4
2	Word choice is original and at times adventurous	Level 3	Level 4
3	Complex sentences are used	Level 3	Level 4
4	Spelling, including longer words with regular spelling patterns, is accurate	Level 3	Level 4
5	Full stops, capital letters and question marks are used correctly	Level 3	Level 4
6	Some sentences have punctuation within the sentence	Level 3	Level 4
7	The style of writing matches the needs of a discursive essay	Level 4	Level 5
8	Word choice is imaginative and words are chosen for precise meanings	Level 4	Level 5
9	The essay is set out in paragraphs with one main topic for each paragraph	Level 4	Level 5
10	Spelling, including words with complex but regular patterns, is usually accurate	Level 4	Level 5
11	Commas, apostrophes and inverted commas are usually used accurately	Level 4	Level 5
12	The style of writing matches the task	Level 5	Level 6
13	A range of words is used to create particular effects	Level 5	Level 6
14	A range of sentence structures is used to create particular effects	Level 5	Level 6
15	Spelling, including that of irregular words, is generally accurate	Level 5	Level 6
16	A range of punctuation is usually used correctly to make the meaning clear	Level 5	Level 6
17	Writing is confident and uses an appropriate style	Level 6	Level 7
18	Ideas are well organised, logical and consistent	Level 6	Level 7
19	Use of words and grammar is accurate and effective	Level 6	Level 7
20	Spelling, including that of irregular words, is accurate	Level 6	Level 7
21	Paragraphing is used to make the sequence of ideas clear and logical for the reader	Level 6	Level 7
22	Correct punctuation is used to help clarify meaning	Level 6	Level 7

7 Creating drama
Cyclops

Your focus

The content of this unit is designed to:
- develop your skills in reading, writing and performing playscripts.

Your target

By the end of this unit you should be more able to:
- read a playscript with appropriate expression
- understand some of the choices playwrights make
- write a playscript using a suitable layout
- use some of the techniques playwrights use to make your own plays effective.

Your move

Speaking and listening

1–2 Preparing and comparing two versions of the arrival of Odysseus

12 Improving your skills in English

Performing dramatic readings

3–4 Preparing and comparing two versions of the arrival of the Cyclops

Self-assessment

Creating drama

5–6 Preparing and comparing two versions of the drunken Cyclops

11 Judging your own performance

Effective playscripts

9 Exploring what makes a good playscript

Exploring playscripts further

8 Exploring the differences between prose and playscript

10 Writing a playscript

7 Comparing three versions of the departure of Odysseus

Performing dramatic readings

The play extracts in this unit are mostly from modern adaptations of the *Odyssey* and they all deal with the story of the Greek hero, Odysseus, and the Cyclops called Polyphemus.

WORDS

▲ **odyssey** *noun* (*plural* odysseys) a long and wandering journey or quest, named after the *Odyssey*, an epic poem by Homer recounting the long wanderings of Odysseus, King of Ithaca in Greek mythology.

1 Preparing two versions of the arrival of Odysseus

▶ In groups, prepare readings of the two extracts below – when Odysseus and his companions arrive on the island of Sicily where the Cyclops lives.

▶ Think about what makes for a good reading, and how you will make your group's performance the best.

▶ Perform these readings to the other groups, concentrating on a powerful reading rather than an acted performance.

ADVICE

As you prepare, consider the following points:
▲ Speaking clearly and coming in on cue.
▲ Deciding the best voice for each particular part in the piece.
▲ Developing a rhythm (e.g. the repetition of 'Imagine a ship' in lines 1–3 of Version 1).
▲ Using the sound of words effectively (e.g. 'wind-crack', 'wave slap', and 'salt-sting' in line 5 of Version 1).
▲ Using the effect of rhyme (e.g. 'night-long, sing-song' in line 30 of Version 1).
▲ Varying how loudly you read each line (e.g. a loud 'Pull... ! Lift... !' in line 7 of Version 1 compared with a quiet 'While they slept I heard it' in line 32).
▲ Making use of stage directions (e.g. the tone of voice suggested by 'Looking around anxiously' in line 52 of Version 2).

Arrival of Odysseus – Version 1

Note: In this version, Odysseus is known as Noman.

A drumbeat begins, slow and steady. A group of five SAILORS, with NOMAN standing central, face outwards. As the SAILORS speak, they mime and enact some of what they describe. For the time being, NOMAN remains still.

1st SAILOR	Imagine a ship.
2nd SAILOR	Imagine a ship on a wide sea.
3rd SAILOR	Imagine a ship on the world-wide, wine-dark sea.
4th SAILOR	A big-bellied sail, creak of timber and rigging.
5th SAILOR	Wind-crack, wave slap, the salt-sting of spray.
1st SAILOR	Hands gripped to the oars...
2nd SAILOR	Pull... ! Lift... ! Drop... ! Pull... !
3rd SAILOR	Shoulders and back muscles strained to breaking!
4th SAILOR	Every bone in the body aching!

5

5th SAILOR	Every nerve and sinew screaming!	10
1st SAILOR	As we ride the ship over the white-topped water...	
2nd SAILOR	Through the whole, deep groaning roll of the ocean.	
3rd SAILOR	Behind us, the sweet incense of war...	
4th SAILOR	A city burned, Troy of the shining towers...	
5th SAILOR	Smoked ruins offered to the bloody mouthed god.	15
1st SAILOR	Ahead of us, an unknown destination...	
2nd SAILOR	Uncharted territories, earth's mystery map.	
3rd SAILOR	Around us, thick night, and a mist filled with moonlight...	
4th SAILOR	Strange lights on the water, a midnight stillness.	
5th SAILOR	And suddenly, there, the sound of breakers!	20
1st SAILOR	And suddenly, there, rising out of the dark...	
2nd SAILOR	The hump-backed crag-black lump of an island!	
3rd SAILOR	And we take the oars and we guide her in...	
4th SAILOR	Hull slapping the shallows...	
5th SAILOR	Keel scraping the gravel...	25
1st SAILOR	Scramble out, drag her safe on to the shore...	
2nd SAILOR	Then stumble up the beach, find shelter in the rocks...	
3rd SAILOR	And drop down worn and exhausted among them...	
4th SAILOR	And sleep all night, our dreams rocking...	
5th SAILOR	To the night-long, sing-song rhyme of the waves.	30
	They sleep. NOMAN speaks to the audience.	
NOMAN	While they slept I heard it. A cry, somewhere above and beyond me, rising up out of the darkness. A wild, inhuman, terrible cry. Like the voice of the monstrous earth itself. It rose, and fell, then rose again, and fell, and rose and fell once more. Three times it sounded, and then it was gone. All night I stood, listening for it, but it never came again.	35

Arrival of Odysseus – Version 2

Note: In this version, the members of the Chorus play the parts of the sons and daughters of Silenus the satyr.

In front of the CYCLOPS' cave.

SILENUS	The Cyclops will be home soon. We must go and milk the ewes.
CHORUS 1	But wait! Look over there. There's a ship drawn up on the shore.
2	Yes, and a party of sailors have disembarked. Who can they be?
3	No visitors come to the island where the Cyclops lives, unless they're mad or lost.
SILENUS	They're carrying bags and water-flasks. They must have stopped to pick up supplies.
CHORUS 4	Don't they know the Cyclops is a man-eating monster who likes nothing better than to feast upon his visitors?
5	They'll find their welcome in the Cyclops' jaws.
6	Quiet! Here they come.

Enter ODYSSEUS, followed by a party of SAILORS.

ODYSSEUS	Greetings, strangers. Can you direct us to a running stream where we may fill our water-flasks? – But what's this I see? Have we come to the country of Dionysus? Unless I'm much mistaken you belong to the satyr race, the goat-footed children of Silenus.
SILENUS	I'll thank you not to mention goats to me. I'm Silenus, as you guessed, and we are satyrs. But though we may have horns and tails, our feet are nothing like a goat's. We may not be men, but we're not beasts either. But who are you, and what are you doing here?
ODYSSEUS	We are Greeks. My name is Odysseus, King of Ithaca.
SILENUS	I've heard of you.
ODYSSEUS	We come from the war at Troy.
SILENUS	So you were involved in that affair, were you? A bad business. Ten years of war, and many thousands slain, all for the sake of one unfaithful wife. And did you get Helen back again?
ODYSSEUS	We sacked the city, and restored her to her husband. Our honour was satisfied.
SILENUS	I'm glad to hear it. But what are you doing here?
ODYSSEUS	Storms drove us off course and scattered our ships. What is this place? Are you the only inhabitants?
SILENUS	These are the slopes of Mount Etna, in Sicily.
ODYSSEUS	Are there no towns or villages on the island?

Line numbers: 5, 10, 15, 20, 25, 30, 35

SILENUS	No men live here.	
ODYSSEUS	Just you and the wild beasts?	
SILENUS	The monsters of the Cyclops race, the sons of Poseidon the god of the sea, inhabit the isle. They don't build towns. They live in caves.	40
ODYSSEUS	Who is their king?	
SILENUS	They haven't got one. There's no government at all. They're utter savages.	
ODYSSEUS	How do they live?	45
SILENUS	They neither farm the land nor follow trades. They keep goats and sheep, and live on cheese and mutton.	
ODYSSEUS	They sound a gentle people. Are they kind to strangers?	
SILENUS	Not really. They think strangers make an excellent meal.	
ODYSSEUS	What? You mean they feed on human flesh?	50
SILENUS	Man-meat, they say, is tenderest of all.	
ODYSSEUS	*(Looking around anxiously)* Where is this Cyclops? Is he near?	
SILENUS	He's gone out hunting, but he'll soon be back. He'll be very pleased to see you.	55

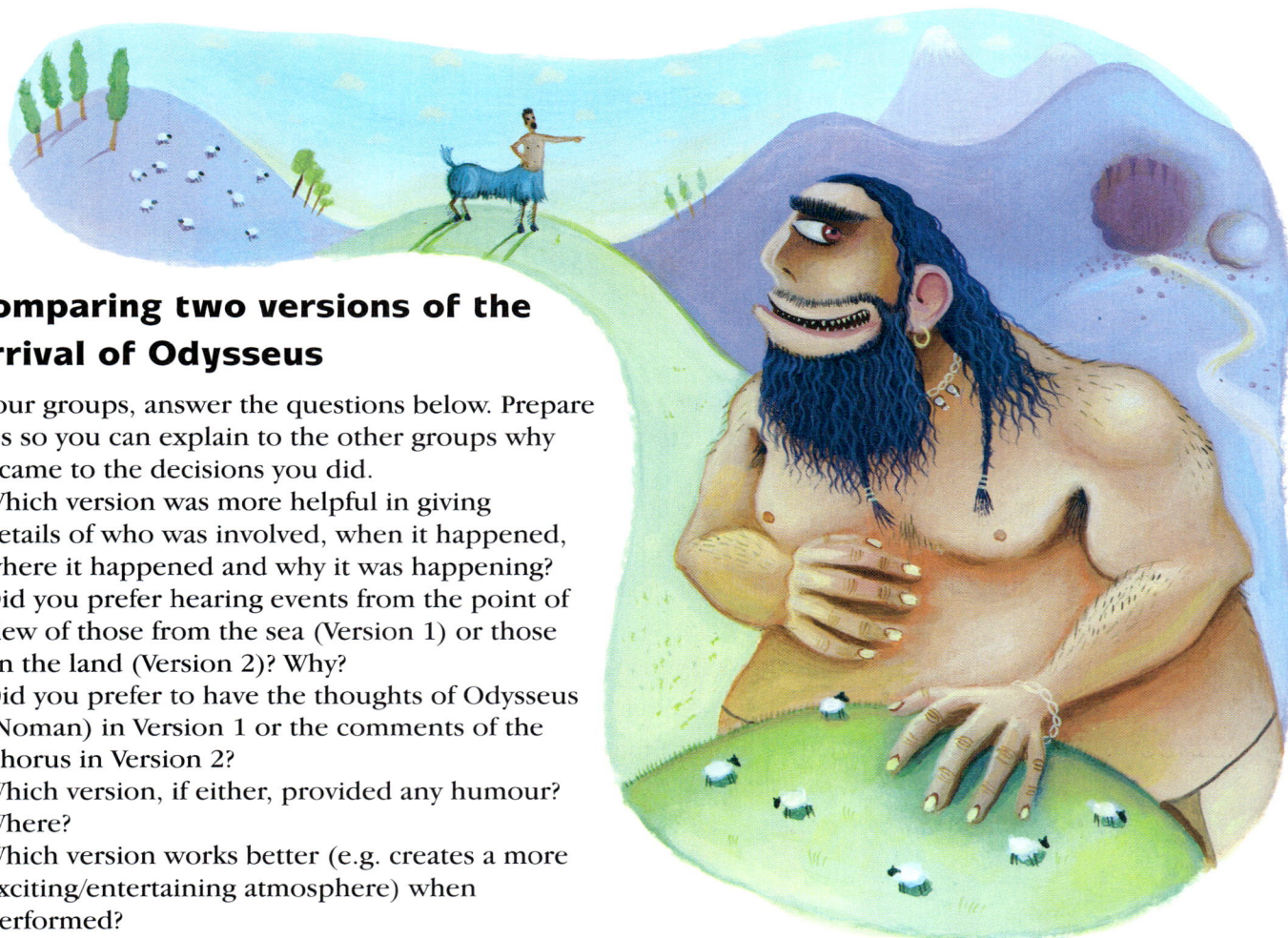

2 Comparing two versions of the arrival of Odysseus

▶ In your groups, answer the questions below. Prepare notes so you can explain to the other groups why you came to the decisions you did.

a Which version was more helpful in giving details of who was involved, when it happened, where it happened and why it was happening?

b Did you prefer hearing events from the point of view of those from the sea (Version 1) or those on the land (Version 2)? Why?

c Did you prefer to have the thoughts of Odysseus (Noman) in Version 1 or the comments of the Chorus in Version 2?

d Which version, if either, provided any humour? Where?

e Which version works better (e.g. creates a more exciting/entertaining atmosphere) when performed?

3 Preparing two versions of the arrival of the Cyclops

▶ In your groups, prepare and perform readings of the two extracts below – when the Cyclops arrives back at his cave.

▶ For this dramatic reading, make use of any good ideas the other groups had in performing the versions of the arrival of Odysseus.

ADVICE

Think about:
▲ speed of delivery (e.g. slow in lines 1–3 of Version 1, then building tension and speed in lines 5–11).
▲ how to show the contrast between the beginning and end of Odysseus's first speech (lines 6–12 of Version 2).
▲ what tone of voice to use for the Cyclops (will you want the audience to sympathise with the Cyclops?).
▲ what the playwrights intended by the use of CAPITALS and *italics* (e.g. 'ROOOOAAAAARRRRR!' in line 22 of Version 1, and 'Oh, *that* food!' in line 34 of Version 2).

Arrival of the Cyclops – Version 1

	SAILORS speak to the audience.	
1st SAILOR	So we stay.	
2nd SAILOR	And we wait.	
3rd SAILOR	There in the dark.	
	Slow drumbeat begins.	
4th SAILOR	Till we hear the sound of goats bleating outside…	5
5th SAILOR	And footsteps on the path, climbing up…	
1st SAILOR	Big, heavy, ground-shaking footsteps…	
2nd SAILOR	And they're getting nearer…	
3rd SAILOR	And the goats come flocking in…	
4th SAILOR	And this huge shadow blocks out the light…	10
5th SAILOR	And we scatter!	
	The SAILORS and NOMAN scatter as the drumbeat rises to a crashing crescendo on the entrance of POLYPHEMOS, a terrible, giant creature with a single, red, staring eye in the middle of its head.	15
1st SAILOR	He stands before us, a monster of a man!	
2nd SAILOR	Body thick-coated with matted hair!	
3rd SAILOR	And right there in the middle of his face…	
4th SAILOR	A single eye like a blazing furnace…	
5th SAILOR	His whole, huge body the hot, hungry oven…	20
ALL	That opens the doors of its mouth and…	
POLYPHEMOS	ROOOOAAAAARRRRR!	
	POLYPHEMOS grabs two of the SAILORS and drags them off as other sailors narrate.	

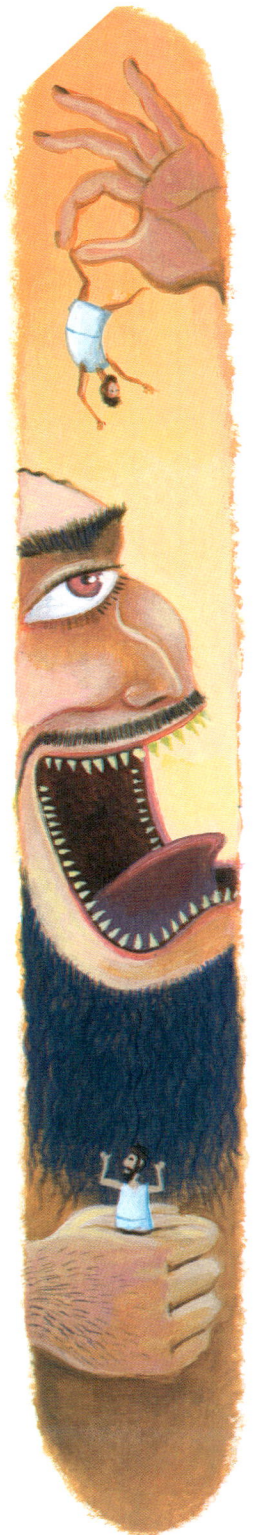

1st SAILOR	Then this creature grabs two of us…	25
2nd SAILOR	One in each hand…	
3rd SAILOR	Smashes their brains out against a rock…	
1st SAILOR	Stuffs them into his mouth, gulps them down…	
2nd SAILOR	Rolls a great stone across the entrance…	
3rd SAILOR	And lies down among his goats, and sleeps.	30

Having eaten the two sailors, POLYPHEMOS lies down and sleeps. The surviving sailors crouch in fear. NOMAN speaks to the audience.

NOMAN   I saw it all. I watched it happen. And though it was terrible, it came as no surprise. When I'd heard those cries the night before, I'd known they were calling us to something like this. As clearly as if the gods had spoken. For they're hostile to us, mean us only harm. When they call, it's to doom and the dark. And when they do, you'd best whistle, and trust in your own hands.

(35)

Arrival of the Cyclops – Version 2

Enter SILENUS with some food.

SILENUS	Well, here's the food.
ODYSSEUS	At last! I'm starving. Quickly – give it here.
SILENUS	But wait! Look over there! The Cyclops is coming! Look out!

The SAILORS run about the stage in panic, while the SATYRS get in their way.

(5)

ODYSSEUS   Quick! We must hide! Don't panic! Come on, run! This way! – No, that way! – No, the other way! – We're trapped! We're done for! – But wait a minute. Stop! *(The SAILORS freeze.)* Is this the way Odysseus should behave? Can a man like me, who fought ten thousand Trojans, turn and run away? Never! I'd disgrace the honour of my fellow Greeks if I was such a coward.

(10)

SILENUS	He's coming!
ODYSSEUS	But, on second thoughts, the wisest thing to do is run and hide. Quick! Into the cave!

(15)

ODYSSEUS and the SAILORS run into the cave. Enter the CYCLOPS.

CYCLOPS   What are you doing standing here? Have you milked my ewes? Are the goats penned up for the night? Are the new-born lambs nuzzling their mothers, drinking their sweet milk? Have you made the cheese and churned the butter? Is my dinner ready?

(20)

SILENUS	Yes, everything's in order. Why don't you go for a nice stroll before supper?
CYCLOPS	I don't want to. I'm hungry. Where's my dinner? In the cave?
SILENUS	No, no! Don't go in there!
CYCLOPS	Why not?
SILENUS	Come over here and admire the view.

(25)

CYCLOPS	What's the matter with you? – *(Noticing the food which SILENUS brought)* What's this food doing here?	
SILENUS	What food?	
CYCLOPS	That food!	30
SILENUS	I can't see anything.	
CYCLOPS	Of course you can! – That food. What's it doing here? Have you been trying to rob me? – Answer, or I'll smash your skull.	
SILENUS	Oh, *that* food! – Well, it wasn't me. My sons and daughters must have done it.	35
CHORUS 1	No, we didn't!	
2	It was him!	
3	We saw him do it!	
CYCLOPS	I'll beat his brains out!	
SILENUS	No! I've just remembered. – I was protecting it from thieves. Some sailors came to rob you, but I wouldn't let them.	40
CYCLOPS	Sailors?	
SILENUS	Greeks from the war at Troy. They said that they'd steal everything you own, but I stood up to them. I fought them single-handed and wouldn't let them take a thing. You wouldn't believe the trouble I go to on your behalf.	45
CYCLOPS	How dare they? Where have they gone?	
SILENUS	I told them you'd be angry, but they said they didn't care, and called you – please forgive me for repeating it – an ugly, savage brute. They said they'd like to cut your ugly throat – their words, not mine – and flay your hide, and squeeze your guts out through your single eye, and do all sorts of nasty things which I'll refrain from mentioning. I told them you'd be cross.	50
CYCLOPS	Where are they? – Light the fire. I'll slaughter them and eat them up at once.	55
SILENUS	Using my cunning, I managed to get them all into your cave. They can't escape.	
CYCLOPS	*(Calling)* You there! Come out. I'm going to eat you.	

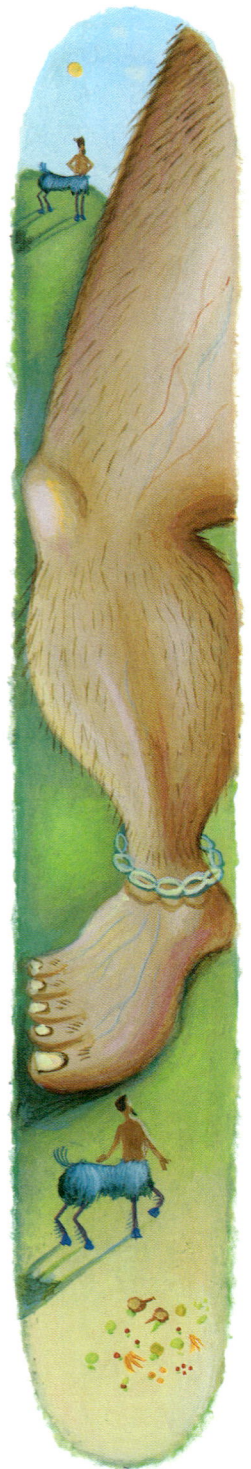

(4) Comparing two versions of the arrival of the Cyclops

▶ In your groups, answer the questions below. Prepare notes so you can explain to the other groups why you came to the decisions you did.

a Which version builds up suspense more effectively?

b Do you prefer the performers to speak to the audience directly (as in Version 1) or pretend the audience is not there (Version 2)? Why?

c Which version uses more comedy? Does it make the performance better?

d Which version develops characters as individuals in a more interesting way? How?

e Which version works better when performed?

5 Preparing two versions of the drunken Cyclops

▶ In your groups, prepare and perform readings of the two extracts below.

▶ Now that you are used to working in a group, you should be able to make your decisions far more quickly and effectively.

▶ Spend just five minutes deciding who should read what parts. Then concentrate on how to read your own part in the most effective way.

▶ When you have completed your performance, reflect on how well you think you worked as a group in both the planning and the performance. Come to an agreement as a group about how you could improve on each in the future.

ADVICE

Discuss with others in your group anything which needs a joint decision, for example:
▲ those playing Polyphemos and Noman in Version 1 need to work together, thinking particularly about the tone of voice to choose around line 8 ('Goat's milk! Is that all?) to make the reading powerful and interesting.
▲ those playing Odysseus and the Cyclops in Version 2 need to decide what tone of voice to use around lines 13 ('No, don't do that') and 37 ('You're very kind').

The drunken Cyclops – Version 1

	NOMAN jumps to his feet and approaches POLYPHEMOS.	
NOMAN	Hey, you! Round-Eye! Cyclops. What's your name?	
POLYPHEMOS	My name? What do you want to know that for?	
NOMAN	If I'm going to be eaten by you, you could at least do me the honour of telling me your name.	
POLYPHEMOS	You're going to be eaten, all right. Eaten by Polyphemos. That's my name.	5
NOMAN	Well, Polyphemos. Haven't you got anything to wash your meal down with?	
POLYPHEMOS	Of course I have. Goat's milk.	
NOMAN	Goat's milk! Is that all?	
POLYPHEMOS	What's wrong with goat's milk?	
NOMAN	Nothing. If you haven't got anything better.	10
POLYPHEMOS	And have you got something better?	
NOMAN	It just so happens I have. Wine.	
	He unties a skin-bag of wine from his belt and holds it up.	
POLYPHEMOS	Wine? What's that? Never heard of it. Is it good to drink?	
NOMAN	Why don't you try it? See what you think.	15
	NOMAN hands the bag of wine to POLYPHEMOS. He drinks from it.	
POLYPHEMOS	It's delicious! Wonderful! So smooth and sweet!	
	It's nectar from heaven, a tasty treat!	
	I've tasted nothing like this before.	
	Now it's all gone, and I want some more.	20
	More! More! MOre! MOre! MORE!	
NOMAN	Of course. Be my guest. Have as much as you like.	
	NOMAN passes another wineskin across. POLYPHEMOS drinks again as the SAILORS speak.	
1st SAILOR	So the Cyclops drinks some more.	25
2nd SAILOR	And it goes straight to his head.	
3rd SAILOR	And by this time he's staggering about the cave.	
1st SAILOR	Flushed and befuddled, and roaring out.	
	POLYPHEMOS sways from side to side and speaks drunkenly.	
POLYPHEMOS	You've made me a gift, now I'll do the same.	30
	All you've got to do is tell me your name.	

NOMAN	Certainly. My name's Noman. That's what everybody calls me. Noman.
POLYPHEMOS	Noman, here's my gift for my favourite guest. I won't eat you now, but you'll be last, and best! *He laughs, then stamps about the stage in a kind of drunken, staggering dance, accompanied by a drumbeat.*

The drunken Cyclops – Version 2

The CYCLOPS enters from the cave. He is drunk.

CYCLOPS	What are you doing out here? Where's that wine? I want more wine.
ODYSSEUS	Here it is. There's plenty left.
CYCLOPS	*(Drinking)* I've never known drink like it. What did you say that god was called whose spirit is in wine?
ODYSSEUS	Dionysus.
CYCLOPS	What sort of god is he?
ODYSSEUS	Giver of heaven's best gifts to humankind.
CYCLOPS	I drank him and he tasted very good. But why does he live inside a skin?
ODYSSEUS	That is his temple. He doesn't mind where he lives.
CYCLOPS	I don't like the skin, but I like what's inside.
ODYSSEUS	Then drink some more.
CYCLOPS	I know what I'll do. I'll invite my brother Cyclops to join me in a drink.
ODYSSEUS	No, don't do that.
CYCLOPS	Why not? I want to share it with my friends.
ODYSSEUS	If you share it there'll be less for you.
CYCLOPS	But I feel happy and I want to see my friends. It would be more fun to drink with others.
ODYSSEUS	But they'll take all the wine, and leave you with nothing.
CYCLOPS	That's true. What should I do?
SILENUS	Stay here, and drink more wine.
CYCLOPS	Perhaps I should. And anyway my legs feel rather funny. I think it would be nice to sit down. *(He sits down suddenly.)* This seems a pleasant spot.
	SILENUS takes the wine-skin and cup from ODYSSEUS, and sits next to the CYCLOPS.
SILENUS	Here, Cyclops, let me pour you out some more.
CYCLOPS	Go ahead.
SILENUS	I'll just taste it to make sure it's all right.
CYCLOPS	Give it here. Put it in the middle where I can see it. – You, stranger, what's your name?
ODYSSEUS	My name is Nobody.
CYCLOPS	Well, Nobody, you're my friend. To thank you for this wine I'm going to give you a reward.
ODYSSEUS	What's that?
CYCLOPS	I won't eat you until I've eaten every one of your companions. I'll save you to the last.
ODYSSEUS	You're very kind.

5

10

15

20

25

30

35

6 Comparing two versions of the drunken Cyclops

▶ In your groups, answer the questions below. Prepare notes so you can explain to the other groups why you came to the decisions you did.
   a Which version makes the Cyclops out to be more threatening and dangerous? How?
   b Which version creates more of a sense of atmosphere (e.g. tension or humour)?
   c Which version shows the effect of drink on the Cyclops more effectively? How?
   d Which version works better when performed?

Exploring playscripts further

7 Comparing three versions of the departure of Odysseus

▶ Read the three extracts below – when Odysseus and his companions leave Sicily.
▶ Without preparing readings, decide which you think makes the most effective ending and why.
▶ Are any of these endings happy endings? Who for?
▶ Do any of these endings make you feel sorry for the Cyclops? How?
▶ Which version creates the best sense of atmosphere (e.g. sad, happy, ominous)?
▶ Which version do you think would work best when performed? Why?

The departure of Odysseus – Version 1

NOMAN	As we pulled away, I looked back, and saw him, standing on the mountain-top. The sun was above him, and he was lit by its golden light, and he lifted his great, round, blind eye to heaven, and cried out. *POLYPHEMOS calls out.*
POLYPHEMOS	Father, Poseidon, Earth-Shaker! Hear my prayer! Take revenge on the man who has wounded and maimed me. Turn the waves against this Noman. Ravage his ship with stormwinds. Let the whole ocean become his enemy, And death stalk him over the wide sea-ways. Hear me, Poseidon. Grant this prayer. For you are my father, and I am your son.
1st SAILOR	His words crash like a curse upon us, their doom's drum sounds in the ocean's deep.
2nd SAILOR	And we feel the sky's weight gathered above, and the weight of the world grinding under our feet.
3rd SAILOR	And from that day on trouble rides in our wake, and we wander the waves like rootless orphans.
1st SAILOR	God-hunted, outcast…
2nd SAILOR	Refugee renegades…
3rd SAILOR	Marked for disaster and nameless death…
1st SAILOR	No place to rest, no shelter or sanctuary…
2nd SAILOR	For Noman's our captain.
3rd SAILOR	And nowhere's our home.

The departure of Odysseus – Version 2

ODYSSEUS	Here I am, Cyclops, safe and sound, Odysseus, King of Ithaca.
CYCLOPS	What's that? Odysseus – I recognise your voice. You're Nobody. What's this new name of yours?
ODYSSEUS	Odysseus. The name my father gave me. Now you see how those who feed upon human flesh are punished.
CYCLOPS	Then the oracle is fulfilled that prophesied that I would lose my eye to someone called Odysseus, coming from Troy. I thought that it would be a giant, mighty and powerful, who would come against me, but you, a miserable and feeble man, have conquered me with wine and blinded me.
ODYSSEUS	It's no more than you deserve.
CYCLOPS	But yet the oracle foretold that you would not escape punishment. It is decreed that you will wander far and wide across the stormy seas and never find your family or your home till ten long years have passed and you've become a stranger in your own land.
ODYSSEUS	What do I care for your oracles? What's done is done. Now we'll leave you to your savage ways and return to Greece.
ODYSSEUS and the SAILORS go off.
SILENUS	Goodbye, Cyclops. We're taking your sheep with us, and we'll think of you each time we slaughter one.
CYCLOPS	No, not my sheep! What will I live on?
SILENUS	You should have thought of that before.
CYCLOPS	I'll be revenged! You won't escape! I'll kill you all! *(Stumbling around blindly)* Where are you?
CHORUS 1	Over here!
CYCLOPS	*(Moving towards the voice)* Where?
CHORUS 2	*(From the other side of the stage)* Behind you!
CYCLOPS	Here?
CHORUS 3	No, over here.
CYCLOPS	You're making fun of me.
The SATYRS dance around the CYCLOPS, keeping just out of reach.
CHORUS 4	You'll never catch us!
5	Just you try!
6	We're free!
1	We're on our way!
2	And now we'll laugh and dance and sing
To celebrate this day.
3	We'll leave this brute to shout and curse.
4	And moan and wail and weep.
5	With any luck he'll starve to death
Without his precious sheep.
SILENUS	A savage monster such as him
Will always get a beating
When he takes on a clever man,
For men are best at cheating.
CYCLOPS	I'll be revenged! I'll get you yet!
Where are you? Come back here!
CHORUS 6	You must be joking!
1	Not a chance!
2	It's time to disappear.
3	Our days of slavery are past.
4	The monster's going to miss us.
ALL	Now all we'll do is drink good wine
And dance with Dionysus!
And, so saying, SILENUS and the CHORUS dance around the stage and off, while the CYCLOPS stumbles off in the wrong direction.

The departure of Odysseus – Version 3

Note: This version is from *The Cyclops* by the ancient Greek playwright Euripides, translated into English by Roger Lancelyn Green.

POLYPHEMUS	Alas, the oracle foretold it right: Which said that you would rob me of my sight Returning home from Troy... It also told Of punishment for being overbold; How, for your cruel deed in blinding me, For long you'd wander homeless on the sea.
ODYSSEUS	I bid you weep! I have done what you say! Think of us sailing on our homeward way Leaving your land of Sicily behind.
POLYPHEMUS	I may prevent it still, although I'm blind! I know another path down to the beach Which I can find by groping. If I reach The place in time, I'll see if showers of stones Can sink your ship, and break your hateful bones!

POLYPHEMUS goes blundering away on one side. ODYSSEUS restrains the SATYRS, silencing them and marshalling them in dumb show – SILENUS, still rather drunk, imitating his actions with ludicrous self-importance. When POLYPHEMUS is well out of sight, ODYSSEUS gives the signal, and sets off in the other direction, followed by his sailors, the SATYRS, and last of all SILENUS, fighting an imaginary rear-guard action. As they go, the SATYRS break into song, SILENUS trying vainly to restrain them.

CHORUS	Hip, hip, hurray! We're on our way As ship-mates of the Ithacan! And happy days We'll pass in praise Extolling Bacchus with a can!

(Exeunt)

8. Exploring the differences between prose and playscript

▶ Read the prose passage below – in which Odysseus is describing his encounter with the Cyclops. The extract comes from a translation of Homer's *Odyssey* (a poem written in Greek) by T E Lawrence.

▶ What are the differences between a prose text like this and a play version?

ADVICE

Think about:
▲ where characters are first named.
▲ how the setting is described.
▲ what happens to inverted commas for speech.
▲ how we know who is speaking.
▲ how we can find out the tone of voice of a speaker.
▲ how we know what happens on stage (e.g. who enters and exits).
▲ whose point of view we hear in a play.

'"Cyclops, you ask me for my public name: I will confess it to you aloud, and do you then give me my guest-gift, as you have promised. My name is No-man: so they have always called me, my mother and father and all my friends."

'I spoke, and he answered from his cruel heart, "I will eat No-man finally, after all his friends. The others first – that shall be your benefit." He sprawled full-length, belly up, on the ground, lolling his fat neck aside; and sleep that conquers all men conquered him.'

Effective playscripts

9 Exploring what makes a good playscript

▶ Reading playscripts is a good way of finding out what works and does not work.

▶ As a result of your experience in preparing readings, see if you can write down any advice you can give to yourself and others about writing an effective dramascript. Make a note of anything else you noticed in the playscripts that was effective in creating a powerful and interesting reading/performance, using a table like the one below.

▶ Write a set of guidelines giving helpful hints on how to write an effective playscript.

What you have noticed while preparing readings of playscripts	How you can help a reader of your script in this way
Stage directions can tell you where the scene is set, what is happening, and who is doing what on stage	
Choosing the right tone of voice makes the reading come alive	
Varying between loud and quiet sections adds to the interest	
Long speeches by one character are not very common in these extracts	
A reading often works best when there is some tension between characters	

ADVICE

▲ A writer of playscripts is often called a playwright.

WORDS

▲ **wright** *noun* (usually in compounds) a maker, creator or repairer, e.g. *playwright, shipwright*.

10 Writing a playscript

▶ You are now going to write your own playscript – be a playwright – using another Greek legend.

▶ Change the story on the next page into a playscript which can be performed by your group.

▶ Use the guidelines you have produced on writing a playscript.

▶ You will need to leave out a considerable amount of detail. Select what you think is essential first, and then what will be most useful to help an audience understand what is happening.

▶ Aim to use a maximum of two sides of A4, or the equivalent.

ADVICE

Consider:
▲ using a narrator/chorus in some parts, or using characters to tell all the story.
▲ how much information you need to include for the benefit of an audience that may not already know the story.
▲ how you could tell most of the story through speech.
Remember to:
▲ select what you think is essential.
▲ select what an audience needs to know in order to understand what is happening.

ADVICE

Include short, sharp scenes including some or all of the following:
▲ Daedalus thinking aloud that he must escape.
▲ Icarus asking his father what he is doing.
▲ Daedalus warning Icarus that he must tell no one.
▲ Daedalus talking to Icarus as Daedalus becomes the first human ever to fly.
▲ Daedalus giving advice to Icarus about where to fly.
▲ Daedalus and Icarus escaping from Crete – perhaps nearly being caught.
▲ Icarus thinking aloud as he decides to climb higher.
▲ Daedalus regretting what he has done.

The wife of Minos, the great king of Crete, was the mother of a strange monster, half-bull, half-man, who was called the Minotaur. Wishing to hide away this disgrace to his family, Minos employed a famous Greek engineer, Daedalus, to make an enclosure so full of winding and difficult passages that the monster could safely be shut up inside and would never find his way out. So Daedalus constructed the famous labyrinth, a maze of such size and with so many deceptive paths that, when the work was over, he himself could hardly find his way back to the main entrance. Inside this labyrinth the Minotaur was shut up, and another story tells how every year, as part of a tribute owed to Minos, boys and girls from Athens were sent to be devoured by the monster. In the end Theseus, the prince of Athens, with the help of Minos's daughter, Ariadne, killed the Minotaur and found his way back to safety. But this did not happen for about twenty years.

When Daedalus had finished building the labyrinth, he wished to return to his home in Greece, but he was so useful as an inventor that Minos refused to let him go. So he and his son Icarus were compelled to stay in Crete against their will.

Finally Daedalus, hating his long exile and longing more and more to see his native country from which he was cut off by a long stretch of sea, said to himself: 'Though Minos has blocked all my ways of escape by land and by water, there is certainly a way through the sky. That is the way I must go. I admit that he is supreme everywhere else, but he does not rule over the air.'

Then he set his mind to work on problems that had never been thought about before, and succeeded in altering the very nature of things. He took feathers and arranged them in a row, beginning with the smallest ones and putting the bigger ones next, so that they looked as though they had grown in the shape of a wing. He tied the feathers together in the middle with twine, and joined them at the base with wax. Then, when they were arranged and fastened, he gave them all a slight bend, so that they looked exactly like the wings of real birds.

While he was working his son Icarus stood and watched him. Sometimes, laughing, he went chasing after a feather that the passing breeze blew away; sometimes he pressed his thumb into the balls of yellow wax. He did not realize that what he was touching was going to be very dangerous to him, and by his playfulness he kept on interrupting the wonderful work on which his father was engaged.

When Daedalus had given the finishing touches to his invention, he put on his wings, flapped them up and down and hung poised in the air above the ground. Then he gave his son careful instructions about how to fly. 'My advice to you, Icarus,' he said, 'is to fly at a moderate height. If you go too low, the sea-water will weigh the feathers down; if you go too high, the heat of the sun will melt the wax. So you must fly neither too high nor too low. The best thing is to follow me.'

While he gave him this advice, he was fitting the strange new wings to his son's shoulders, and, as he did so, tears ran down his aged cheeks and his hands trembled. He kissed his son for what was fated to be the last time, and then, taking to the air, he flew on ahead, anxious for the boy, like a bird which for the first time leads his fledglings out of their high nest into the yielding air. He called out words of encouragement to the boy and taught him to use those fatal wings, constantly looking back, as he flapped his own wings, to see how his son was managing.

On the ground people fishing with long trembling rods, or shepherds leaning on their crooks, or ploughmen bent over their plough handles looked up at them in astonishment and came to the conclusion that, since they were flying through the air, they must be gods.

At this point the boy began to enjoy the daring experience of flight. Longing for the open sky, he forgot to follow his father and climbed higher and higher in the air. As he came nearer to the sun, the scorching rays began to soften the wax that kept the feathers together. The wax melted and Icarus found that he was flapping bare arms which, without their wings, had no hold upon the air. He fell, and the blue sea, which is still called the Icarian Sea, closed over his lips, as he cried out for his father. Unhappy Daedalus, a father no longer, also cried out. 'Icarus!' he called. 'Where are you? Where have you gone to?' As he was crying out the boy's name, he saw the wings floating on the water. Then he cursed his own invention, found his son's dead body and buried it. The land is still called after the name of the buried boy.

Adapted from The Stories of the Greeks *by Rex Warner*

Self-assessment

11 Judging your own performance

▶ From the list below:

a select three points on which you feel you have made the most progress.

b select one point on which you most need to improve.

I can compare two playscripts and explain which I think is more effective.

I can read a playscript with expression.

I can listen carefully and make fair comments on play readings by other groups.

I can comment on an author's choice of words and the effect they have.

I can write a useful set of guidelines on how to write a playscript.

I can write an effective playscript following these guidelines.

I can work co-operatively in a group, helping the group to focus on the task.

I can make useful suggestions about how the group can work better together next time.

I can select what is essential when re-telling a story in playscript form.

▶ Write down one strategy you could adopt to help you improve on the area you have targeted for improvement.

12 Improving your skills in English

▶ Select one or two skills you need to concentrate on to improve your skills in speaking and listening. (The descriptions of levels are a guide, not a rulebook.)

	Speaking and listening skill	From	To
1	Talk and listen with confidence in an increasing range of contexts	Level 3	Level 4
2	Develop ideas thoughtfully, conveying opinions clearly	Level 3	Level 4
3	Talk and listen confidently in a wide range of contexts	Level 4	Level 5
4	Make contributions which take account of others' views	Level 4	Level 5
5	Adapt talk to the demands of different contexts with increasing confidence	Level 5	Level 6
6	Understand ideas and show sensitivity to others	Level 5	Level 6
7	Show confidence in matching talk to the demands of different contexts	Level 6	Level 7
8	Evaluate others' ideas and vary how and when to participate	Level 6	Level 7
9	Maintain and develop talk in a range of contexts	Level 7	Above Level 7
10	Make a range of contributions which show they have listened perceptively and are sensitive to the development of the discussion	Level 7	Above Level 7

8 Using standard English

Your focus

The content of this unit is designed to:
- improve your skills in using the right kind of language in the right situations.

Your target

By the end of this unit you should be more able to:
- recognise standard and non-standard forms of English
- speak and write standard English more fluently
- choose the most appropriate words and style for a particular context.

Your move

Speaking and listening/writing

Writing

1 Commenting on newspaper articles

2 Recognising abbreviations

3 Recognising standard and non-standard grammar

15 Improving your skills in English

Non-standard English usage

4 Understanding verbs

Self-assessment

Using standard English

5 Exploring variations of dialect

14 Judging your own performance

11 The structure of a newspaper article

Exploring newspaper articles

Discussing context

Exploring dictionaries

8 Creating entries for a dictionary of modern English usage

12 Writing a newspaper article

13 Commenting on your own writing

9 The right words for the right situation

6 What a dictionary includes

7 How a dictionary operates

10 Newspapers – right or wrong?

Messages by mobile ruin children's English

CHILDREN'S writing is becoming worse as e-mail and mobile phone text messaging become more popular. Abbreviations used to save space and time are undermining the correct use of English, say researchers.

Advertising agency McCann-Erickson found children use a mix of numbers, letters and punctuation to replace proper words. The phrase "for you" becomes "4U", and "see you tonight" can read "CU tonite". Youngsters also use icons such as ":-)" – a smiling face which can mean happy or good – and ":-(" – a glum face meaning sad or bad – instead of words. The agency's Robin Lauffer said: "We are witnessing a communications revolution."

From the Daily Express, *2 September 2000*

E-mail sends coded warning to English teachers

By David Charter
Education Correspondent

TEENAGERS' love 4 e-mail is ruining their grammar n will consign the traditional hand-written letter 2 history, researchers said yesterday :-(

Children are inventing a new lexicon for electronic communication with a range of abbreviations and symbols that adults find hard to understand. Although educators and politicians were once most concerned about the sloppy pronunciation associated with "Estuary English", it seems that "E-Mail English" poses a greater threat to the language.

For example, the symbol :-(represents a sad face and is widely used to signify sympathy, disappointment or bad news. The symbols have evolved to keep down the cost of mobile phone text-messaging and e-mailing, speed up the response time and inject emotion into concise missives.

Teachers say that the new shorthand style associated with e-mails is making their job of improving literacy skills even harder.

Researchers from the McCann-Erikson advertising agency, who interviewed more than 100 children aged 5-11, concluded that traditional letter-writing will be of no more use later in life than the history lessons pupils learn in school.

Robin Lauffer, who led the research, said that the symbols used in text messages represented new ways of expressing emotions. "You need intonation if you are going down to the shortest possible form of communication. So if you put a smiley face next to a sarcastic comment, it shows you are joking and not being nasty.

"We are witnessing a communications revolution which children have adapted to very quickly. Our language is changing in front of our eyes."

More than half a billion text messages are sent by mobile phone every month. The growing trend coincides with concern over standards in formal writing. Just 54 per cent of 11-year-olds achieved the expected level in writing in last summer's national tests compared to 78 per cent in reading.

Nigel de Gruchy, general secretary of the NASUWT teachers' union, said that "-Disgusted from Tunbridge Wells" should be more concerned about the influence of e-mail than any failings of teachers. "Dropping grammar and replacing sentences with jargon will damage the language."

Ms Lauffer added: "Kids have always had some coded language of their own which separates them from grown-ups but the Internet and mobile phone has given them the ability to do this much more. Writing a long-hand letter is going to have to be something that is taught in school and, while they will know how to do this, the question is, will they want to?"

From The Times, *2 September 2000*

Non-standard English usage

1 Commenting on newspaper articles

▶ Read the newspaper articles on page 90.

▶ The article from *The Times* says, 'For example, the symbol :-(represents a sad face and is widely used to signify sympathy, disappointment or bad news.' Has *The Times* got it right?

▶ According to the researchers, 'traditional letter-writing will be of no more use later in life than the history lessons pupils learn in school'. Do you agree about letter-writing? Do you agree about history?

▶ Was your reading result higher than your writing result in the last test you did? If so, why do you think this was?

▶ Do you think using e-mail and mobile phones makes your communication skills better or worse? Why?

▶ Newspaper articles usually use standard English. Do these articles use standard English? If not, why not?

▶ Using a flow chart, coloured letters or a design idea of your own, show how the word 'emoticon' has been created from two other words.

2 Recognising abbreviations

▶ List some of the most common abbreviations (shortenings of a word written instead of using the whole word) used in electronic and other texts. Start with the ones used in the newspaper articles on page 90.

▶ Use a table like the one below.

Whole word	Abbreviation/variation
and	
for	
see	
tonight	
you	

WORDS

▲ **emotion** *noun* **1** a strong feeling, e.g. anger, fear, or joy, often involving physiological change, e.g. rise in the pulse rate. **2** instinctive feelings or reactions, especially as opposed to reason. [From the Latin *emovere, emotum* meaning to stir up or disturb.] ('*Symbols used in text messages represented new ways of expressing emotions.*')

▲ **icon** *noun* a pictorial representation; an image or symbol. [From the Greek *eikon* meaning image.] ('*Youngsters also use icons such as ":-)" – a smiling face which can mean happy or good – and ":-(" a glum face meaning sad or bad – instead of words.*')

▲ **emoticon** *noun* a representation of a human face that is formed from keyboard characters and used in e-mail to express feelings (blend of *emotion* and *icon*). (e.g. '*An even quicker way of showing moods and emotions whilst observing etiquette are emoticons.*')

▲ **lexicon** *noun* the vocabulary of a language, individual or subject. [From the Greek *lexis* meaning word, speech.] ('*Children are inventing a new lexicon for electronic communication.*')

3 Recognising standard and non-standard grammar

▶ Write down the standard English forms of these common non-standard forms in a table like the one below.
▶ Choose two or three of these and, for each one, work out and write down a helpful way to remember how to write it in standard English.

Number	Non-standard English	Standard English
1	Come over here quick	
2	I ain't agreeing to that	
3	I didn't do nothing	
4	I done my homework	
5	I seen the video	
6	I were on my own	
7	She went to the film with Craig and I	
8	Susan and me went to the film	
9	Them books are old	
10	We went straight out the door and up town	
11	We was in the shopping centre	

4 Understanding verbs

▶ Verbs such as 'to be', 'to do', 'to go' and 'to see' often cause problems. This may partly be because they are irregular in their patterns. All of these verbs are explored further below, along with some more standard verbs.
▶ Without using a dictionary, fill in a table like the one below. Two examples have been completed for you.

Verb in infinitive (base form)	The -ing participle, e.g. he was going	The -ed participle, e.g. I've kicked the ball	The past tense, e.g. I kicked the ball
be	being	been	was
buy	buying	bought	bought
catch			
communicate			
develop			
do			
eat			
find			
go			
learn			

Verb in infinitive (base form)	The -ing participle, e.g. he was going	The -ed participle, e.g. I've kicked the ball	The past tense, e.g. I kicked the ball
see			
sell			
swim			
teach			
write			

▶ Which of the words in the table follow a regular pattern for the formation of the past tense?

▶ Choose one of the words which follows an irregular pattern and create realistic sentences using the word:

  a as the '-ing participle' (see column 2).
  b as the '-ed participle' (see column 3).
  c in the past tense (see column 4).

5 Exploring variations of dialect

Word	Variations of dialect, etc.	Where used
trainers		
truant		

▶ Using the whole class as a resource, find out how many dialect words you know for the words in the table on the right.

▶ You could also think about what words would be used in soaps from various countries, e.g. Australia and the USA.

▶ Collect examples of non-standard English that you come across. These might be:

  a in conversations you hear.
  b on the radio or television.
  c in books, newspapers and magazines.
  d in any other spoken or written form of English.

▶ Classify them as dialect, informal, slang, etc. (Some dictionaries will give you the classification if you are not sure where they fit in.)

▶ Are any of the uses you come across incorrect uses of English?

▶ Create a mind map that includes standard and non-standard English, types of non-standard English (see activities above), and examples of each type.

WORDS

▲ **colloquial** *adjective* used in familiar conversation rather than in formal speech or writing. For example, 'chuck something out' (get rid of it), 'get into something' (start an interest or hobby). [From the Latin *colloquium* meaning conversation.]

▲ **dialect** *noun* a form of language spoken in a particular region or by a certain social group, differing from other forms in grammar, vocabulary and in some cases pronunciation. For example, regional variations for 'truant'.

▲ **informal** (vocabulary, idiom, etc.) *adjective* appropriate to everyday conversational language rather than to formal written language. For example, 'con' (conman), 'get up and go' (energy, drive or ambition).

▲ **slang** *noun* very informal words; language not accepted for dignified use. For example, 'chuck someone' (abandon a partner), 'a get/git' (a fool).

Note: Some of these descriptions overlap, e.g. some dictionaries say 'get into something' is colloquial, others say it is informal.

Totally wicked

Make growing up easier on everyone, with modern designs they'll love, and room for a sleep-over bed, plus about 50 different nail varnishes. Now that's what they call bad, Mum.

From the IKEA 2001 catalogue. Why do you think IKEA uses non-standard English in this advertisement?

Exploring dictionaries

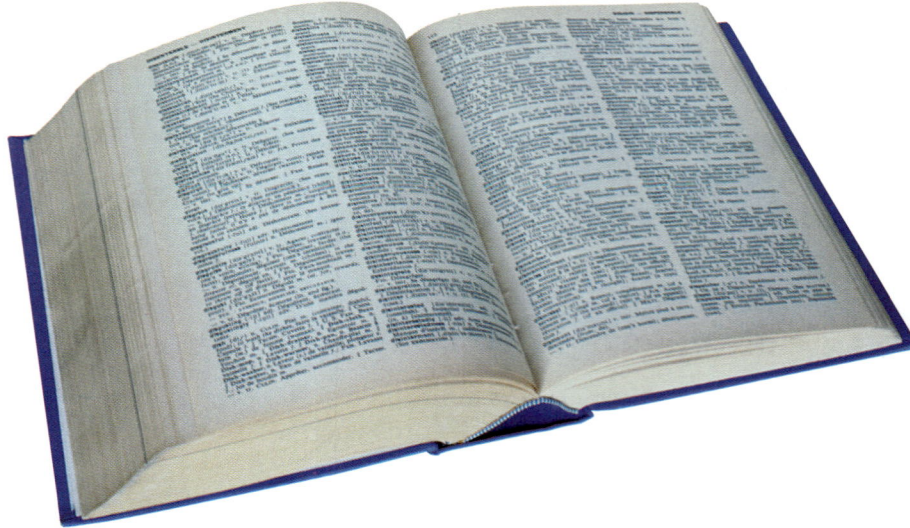

6 What a dictionary includes

▶ Why do you think 'sleep-over' was not included in the 1999 edition of the *Chambers 21st Century Dictionary*? Be ready to explain your reasoning to the rest of the class.

▶ Four possible reasons are listed below. Come up with others if you think these are not the only ones possible.
  a It was a word used only by young people, so the compilers did not think it was a suitable word to include in a dictionary.
  b The word was not common in the UK before 1999, when this edition was published.
  c The word was common, but the compilers had not heard it.
  d The word had not been invented when the dictionary was compiled.

▶ What information does a dictionary include about a word? Look up the following words in a dictionary:
  a Metaphor.
  b Modem.
  c Paragraph.
  d Stanza.

▶ Write down what items of information the dictionary includes for these words, and in what order. Once you have decided, fill in the boxes in a table like the one below. The first item the dictionary includes has been provided for you.

▶ Note that some words do not show up all the possible types of information, but if you look up these four words, most possible examples should be covered.

The word, showing how it is spelt			

7 How a dictionary operates

▶ Look up in your dictionary the two words below:
  a Optimum.   **b** Grab.
▶ Match up the details in the dictionary to the types of information you have already labelled. Some sections may need to be left empty.
▶ You may find you need additional sections when you try this.

optimum			
grab			

WORDS
▲ Meanings change and develop. Over recent decades, words such as 'cool' and 'wicked' have gained additional meanings not listed in older dictionaries. The new meanings may come and go as fashions in language change. New words such as 'sleep-over' also come into the language.

8 Creating entries for a dictionary of modern English usage

▶ Make a list of 20 words that you and your friends know and use, but which are not mentioned in the dictionary in the way you use them.
▶ Select 10 of these words that you will concentrate on. Show your teacher your choices before going on to the next stage.
▶ Create a dictionary entry for each of these 10 words, following exactly the same pattern as you have already identified from published dictionaries.
▶ Follow the same order and format as the dictionary. It may help to look up a verb in the dictionary when you are writing a dictionary entry for a verb, and so on.
▶ Include an example of a typical sentence in which your chosen words would be used. Insert the word 'usage' before any such example.
▶ You may find the following tables useful in selecting abbreviations.

Word class	Abbreviation	Examples
adjective	adj.	awkward, deep, green, holy, lazy, polite
adverb	adv.	amazingly, directly, politely, slowly
noun	n.	book, house, idea, person, tree, wolf
verb	vb.	to demonstrate, to grow, to move, to see, to try

Abbreviation	What it means in a dictionary	Word in full
c.	Tells you which hundred-year period this word was first used in, e.g. 21st-c.	century
colloq.	Tells you that this word is only used in informal situations	colloquial
derog.	Tells you this word is only used when the user wants to insult the person or thing specified	derogatory
esp.	Denotes the most common usage of a word	especially
pl.	Indicates the plural spelling of the word	plural

Discussing context

9 The right words for the right situation

▶ When would it be appropriate to use the kind of words you have included in your dictionary entries?

▶ Make notes in a table like the one below on each of the following to help you prepare for the class discussion which will follow.

Context	Appropriate or not? Give reasons
As part of a discussion in class	
In the explanation part of a dictionary entry	
In a piece of writing where you are asked to use standard English	
In a story where you want to show how your friends actually speak	
In a written essay in school	
In conversation with your friends	
When talking to your headteacher	
When talking to your parents	

10 Newspapers – right or wrong?

▶ Look back at the opinions expressed in the newspaper articles from the *Daily Express* and *The Times* on page 90.

▶ Is it true that modern methods of communication such as e-mails are ruining the way children write?

:-)   ;-)   #-)

:-(%-)

Exploring newspaper articles

The newspaper articles from the *Daily Express* and *The Times* were based on the same press release, which is displayed below.

Press Release
8 August 2000

DU SPK TEXT?
New Report Highlights Latest Language Trends

Kids are taking language to another level. Without teachers and parents to regulate e-mails and text messages on mobiles, kids have ditched time-consuming conventional language. Grammar, traditional spelling and vowels are out; letters, numbers and punctuation are in.

The findings are from the latest report from McCann Junior, ad agency McCann-Erickson's strategic planning unit dedicated solely to kids. Various elements of kid culture are examined to help understand more about this elusive consumer group and anticipate trends.

'We are witnessing a communications revolution which kids have adapted to very quickly. Our language is changing in front of our eyes,' says Robin Lauffer, McCann-Erickson UK & Ireland Executive Planning Director.

Kids live their lives on the move and rely on *quick* communication. The mobile is key. Kids as young as six have colourful Motorolas tucked away in custom-built phone pouches. Text messaging has revolutionised the way kids commune, superseding scribbled notes in class.

Although brevity is all, there are unspoken rules. Never forget the question or exclamation marks, because in the absence of words, they set the tone. Traditional pleasantries are still observed, but they have been re-invented because the old ones took too long. Nicknames have been shortened, now it's just the first letter and a kiss for good luck – sxx. This is not perceived as rude. Kids understand the pressure of time.

An even quicker way of showing moods and emotions whilst observing etiquette are emoticons. A few examples:

:-)	I'm smiling, happy to see you, it's a joke
:-(	I'm unhappy, sorry
;-)	Wink, wink, just joking, I'm flirting with you
%-)	I'm funny looking, I wear glasses, I'm crazy
#-)	I'm drunk, have a headache, I'm confused

'This language can look like code to an outsider, but it will have a significant effect on our language as kids continue this shorthand to adulthood,' concludes Lauffer.

ENDS

11 The structure of a newspaper article

▶ You will now be preparing to write your own newspaper article, using standard English. To help you make it realistic, you will be exploring first how published articles are written.

▶ Look back at the two newspaper articles on page 90 and, using a table like the one below, decide how they are similar.

Structure	
What comes first	
What the first paragraph is about/what the first paragraph does	
Layout of text	
How the first word of the article is written	
How the article ends	
Content	
What quotation they both use	
The source for the findings	
What examples they give from the press release	

▶ Now identify at least four things that are different, using a table like the one below.

	Daily Express	The Times
Naming of journalist		
Length of report		
Width of columns		
Using sources other than the press release		
Any other differences you notice		

▶ Try to explain why you think the two newspapers chose different approaches.

WORDS

▲ **byline** *noun* **1** *journalism* a line under the title of a newspaper or magazine article which gives the name of the author. **2** *football* the touchline.

12 Writing a newspaper article

▶ You will now be writing your own newspaper article on the same topic. You have exactly the same press release the journalists from the *Daily Express* and *The Times* had (see page 97).

▶ First of all, decide which type of newspaper you will be writing for:
  a One similar to the *Daily Express*.
  b One similar to *The Times*.
  c One aimed at your age group.

▶ Then, read the press release on page 97 again and decide if you are going to:
  a write an article that does not take sides (so you will use quotations from both sides of the argument).
  b say that new technology is ruining children's English (so you will use only quotations that support this point of view).
  c say that the new technology is allowing children to communicate far more (so you will use only quotations that support this point of view).

▶ Now, obtain quotations from fellow pupils/parents/teachers to include in your article.

▶ Finally, write your newspaper article in no more than 300 words, making it look and read just like an actual newspaper article.

ADVICE

▲ The headline must sum up in very few words the line of argument you will take.
▲ The introductory paragraph must lure and hook the reader.
▲ Within the first two paragraphs, include as far as possible:
  • who – the age group involved
  • what – the cause of all the concern
  • when – how long this has been a problem
  • why – the reasons for it happening
  • where – what parts of the country/world are involved
  • how – how it came to affect this age group so much.
▲ In the next paragraph, you could say what the consequences are/use quotations.
▲ In the final paragraphs, use quotations and come to some definite ending.
▲ You should remember that the newspaper editor may use only the first two paragraphs of your article. Have you included all the key news points in this opening section?
▲ Remember that if you want to take sides in your article, you can simply use the quotations from people you agree with and ignore any others. Do include your own ideas, but make it read like a real newspaper article.

13 Commenting on your own writing

▶ Newspaper articles are usually written in standard English. Have you used standard English all through your article? If not, why not?

▶ Write a short note to the person who will be marking your work, explaining if you have used any non-standard English, and, if so, why.

Self-assessment

14 Judging your own performance

▶ From the list below:
    a select three points on which you feel you have made the most progress.
    b select one point on which you most need to improve.
    I can write a dictionary entry that looks exactly like a published version.
    I can recognise words that are not standard English.
    I know when it is appropriate to use standard English.
    I can co-operate with a group and am prepared to follow a group decision, even if it is not my own.
    I know how a typical newspaper article is organised.
    I can write a newspaper article using standard English appropriately.
    I can write a newspaper article which looks and reads like a real newspaper article.

15 Improving your skills in English

▶ Select one or two skills you need to concentrate on to improve your skills in speaking and listening, and writing. Then do the same for your writing skills. (The descriptions of levels are a guide, not a rulebook.)

	Speaking and listening/writing skill	From	To
1	Use some standard English words	Level 3	Level 4
2	Use some standard English grammar	Level 3	Level 4
3	Use some standard English in formal situations	Level 4	Level 5
4	Fluent in use of standard English in formal situations	Level 5	Level 6
5	Confident use of standard English when appropriate	Level 6	Level 7
6	Confident use of standard English in a range of situations, adapting as necessary	Level 7	Above Level 7

	Writing skill	From	To
1	Text set out like a newspaper article	Level 3	Level 4
2	Formal style used if necessary, and words used precisely	Level 4	Level 5
3	Impersonal style used if necessary, and words chosen to create particular effects	Level 5	Level 6
4	Ideas organised and coherent, and words used accurately and effectively	Level 6	Level 7
5	Writing coherent and gives clear point of view if appropriate. Words chosen for very precise effects or for emphasis	Level 7	Above Level 7

9 Reading and writing narrative
Special FX

Your focus

The content of this unit is designed to:
- help you understand the choices authors make to create effects
- give you the skills to use the same techniques yourself.

Your target

By the end of this unit you should be more able to:
- recognise techniques that writers use in narrative
- read a story with appreciation
- write a story of which you are proud.

Your move

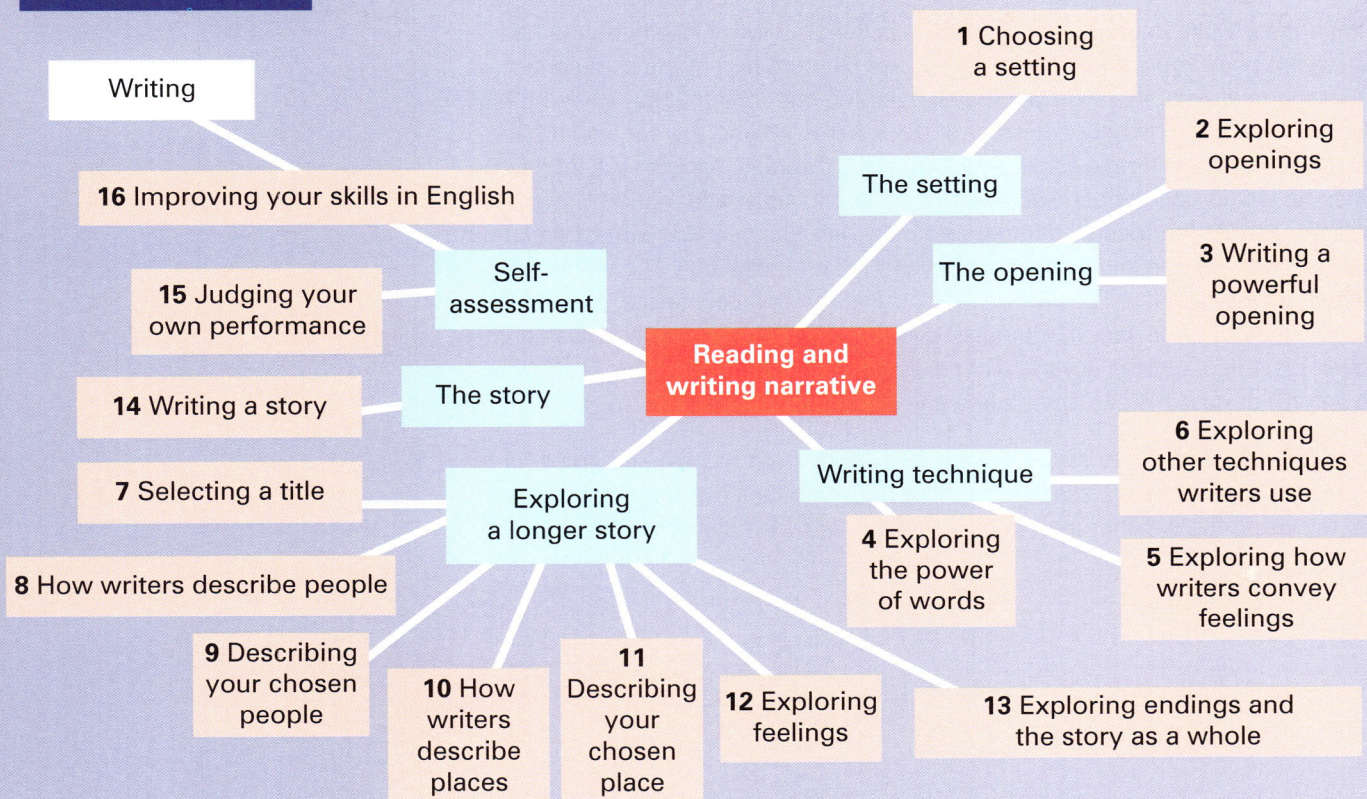

Writing

16 Improving your skills in English

15 Judging your own performance

Self-assessment

14 Writing a story

The story

7 Selecting a title

8 How writers describe people

Exploring a longer story

9 Describing your chosen people

10 How writers describe places

11 Describing your chosen place

12 Exploring feelings

Reading and writing narrative

1 Choosing a setting

The setting

2 Exploring openings

The opening

3 Writing a powerful opening

Writing technique

6 Exploring other techniques writers use

4 Exploring the power of words

5 Exploring how writers convey feelings

13 Exploring endings and the story as a whole

The setting

1 Choosing a setting

▶ By the end of this unit you should have completed a story covering at least three sides of A4 or the equivalent. The story will be based on arriving at a new place for the first time.

▶ You could think about:
   a the first time you went into hospital, either as a patient or visiting.
   b the first time at a new school.
   c the first time you visited a concert hall or sports venue.
   d the first time you remember visiting the dentist.
   e the first time you visited a particular holiday destination.

▶ It is up to you to select a place that you can use as the basis of a good story. As you work through this unit you will gradually be building up your story, so it would be a good idea to work out now your two or three favourite choices of place for the activities which follow.

▶ Write down up to three possible places for the setting of your story.

ADVICE

▲ Base your story on an actual event (although you may wish to change the details to make the story more powerful and effective).

The opening

2 Exploring openings

▶ Read the following extract from *The Daydreamer* by Ian McEwan.

When Peter woke in the morning, he always kept his eyes closed until he had answered two simple questions. They always came to him in the same order. Question one: who am I? Oh yes, Peter, aged ten and a half. Then, still with his eyes closed, question two: what day of the week is it? And there it would be, a fact as solid and as immoveable as a mountain. Tuesday. Another school day. 5
Then he would pull the blankets over his head and sink deeper into his own warmth and let the friendly darkness swallow him up. He could almost pretend he did not exist. But he knew he would have to force himself out. The whole world agreed it was Tuesday. The earth itself, hurtling through cold space, spinning and revolving around the sun, had brought everyone to Tuesday and there was nothing 10
Peter, his parents or the government could do to change the fact. He would have to get up, or miss his bus and be late and get into trouble.

How cruel it was then to drag his warm dozy body from its nest and grope for his clothes, knowing that in less than an hour he would be shivering at the bus stop. On television the weather man had said that it was the coldest for fifteen years. 15

Cold, but no fun. No snow, no frost, not even an icy puddle to skate on. Only cold and grey, with a bitter wind that reached into Peter's bedroom through a crack in the window. There were times when it seemed to him that all he had ever done in his life, and all he was ever going to do, was wake up, get up, and go to school. It did not make it easier that everyone else, grown-ups included, had to get up on dark winter mornings. If only they would all agree to stop, then he could stop too. But the earth kept turning, Monday, Tuesday, Wednesday came round again, and everyone went on getting out of bed.

20

▶ In pairs, select five points about this opening of a story which you think are either good or bad. The five points can be a mixture of both. You should be ready to explain your choice to the other groups.
▶ Use a table like the one below.

	Quotation	What makes it good/bad/ effective/ineffective
1		
2		
3		
4		
5		

3 Writing a powerful opening

▶ The obvious way to start a story is to describe getting up on the morning of the day you are about to describe. But the reader is not likely to be interested in details such as cleaning your teeth or having breakfast unless it shows what is special about this particular day.
▶ The two essential principles for a good opening are:
  a make this occasion different from any other occasion.
  b hook the reader into the story in some way, e.g. by hinting at what is coming next.
▶ Write the opening paragraph for your story. It will help if you have decided by now on the place you are going to describe your first visit to.

Writing technique

4 Exploring the power of words

▶ Read the following extract from *Northern Lights* by Philip Pullman.
▶ Lyra is having a discussion with a bear called Iorek. In this story, the bear can talk.

'Could the bears ever be defeated, Iorek?'

'No.'

'Or tricked, maybe?'

He stopped gnawing and looked at her directly. Then he said, 'You will never defeat
the armoured bears. You have seen my armour; now look at my weapons.'   5

He dropped the meat and held out his paws, palm upward, for her to look at. Each
black pad was covered in horny skin an inch or more thick, and each of the claws was
as long as Lyra's hand at least, and as sharp as a knife. He let her run her hands over
them wonderingly.

'One blow will crush a seal's skull,' he said. 'Or break a man's back, or tear off a   10
limb. And I can bite. If you had not stopped me in Trollesund, I would have crushed
that man's head like an egg. So much for strength; now for trickery. You cannot trick
a bear. You want to see proof? Take a stick and fence with me.'

Eager to try, she snapped a stick off a snow-laden bush, trimmed all the side-shoots
off, and swished it from side to side like a rapier. Iorek Byrnison sat back on his   15
haunches and waited, forepaws in his lap. When she was ready she faced him, but she
didn't like to stab at him because he looked so peaceable. So she flourished it, feinting
to right and left, not intending to hit him at all, and he didn't move. She did that
several times, and not once did he move so much as an inch.

Finally she decided to thrust at him directly, not hard, but just to touch the stick to his
stomach. Instantly his paw reached forward and flicked the stick aside.   20

Surprised, she tried again, with the same result. He moved far more quickly and
surely than she did. She tried to hit him in earnest, wielding the stick like a fencer's
foil, and not once did it land on his body. He seemed to know what she intended
before she did, and when she lunged at his head, the great paw swept the stick aside   25
harmlessly, and when she feinted, he didn't move at all.

She became exasperated, and threw herself into a furious attack, jabbing and lashing
and thrusting and stabbing, and never once did she get past those paws. They moved
everywhere, precisely in time to parry, precisely at the right spot to block.

Finally she was frightened, and stopped. She was sweating inside her furs, out of   30
breath, exhausted, and the bear still sat impassive. If she had had a real sword with a
murderous point, he would have been quite unharmed.

'I bet you could catch bullets,' she said, and threw the stick away. 'How do you *do*
that?'

'By not being human,' he said. 'That's why you could never trick a bear. We see   35
tricks and deceit as plain as arms and legs. We can see in a way that humans have
forgotten.'

▶ You will be allocated a colour for this activity:
  a Red relates to modifiers such as adjectives and adverbs.
  b Green relates to nouns, including proper nouns.
  c Blue relates to verbs.
▶ Your task is to convince the other groups that 'your' colour words are the most
  important.
▶ Select five or so of your colour words that you think are particularly effective. Be
  ready to justify your opinion to the other groups that your words are the most
  important in the passage.
▶ Look back at a recent piece of your own writing. Try to work out if you need to
  include more modifiers, nouns or verbs, or if you have got the balance about right.

5 Exploring how writers convey feelings

▶ The quotations selected below tell you something about a character's
  feelings without saying directly what those feelings are.
▶ In each case, explain what you think that character is feeling, and how
  you can tell this. Use a table like the one below.

Line	Quotation	What the character is thinking/feeling	How you can tell this
4	He stopped gnawing and looked at her directly		
30	She was sweating inside her furs		
33	and threw the stick away		

▶ What can you tell about Lyra's feelings from the way she asks the
  question, 'How do you *do* that?' (lines 33–34)? You will need to explain
  your reasons.

6 Exploring other techniques writers use

▶ Why do you think Philip
  Pullman chose to use
  two questions from Lyra
  at the start of this
  extract? Think about:
  a what the questions
    tell you about Lyra.
  b how you may read
    the rest of the extract
    differently after
    reading the questions.

Exploring a longer story

7 Selecting a title

▶ Read the following short story by Penelope Lively. The story has been printed with the title removed.

▶ Decide in your group what you think would be the best title and why.

▶ After you have heard the titles from the other groups, choose what you think is the best of all the suggestions.

▶ When you have heard the author's title, decide if you think it is better than your final choice and why.

Inside the car it was quiet, the noise of the engine even and subdued, the air just the right temperature, the windows tight-fitting. The boy sat on the back seat, a box of chocolates, unopened, beside him, and a comic, folded. The trim Sussex landscape flowed past the windows: cows, white-fenced fields, highly-priced period houses. The sunlight was glassy, remote as a coloured photograph. The backs of the two heads in front of him swayed with the motion of the car.   5

His mother half-turned to speak to him. 'Nearly there now, darling.'

The father glanced down at his wife's wrist. 'Are we all right for time?'

'Just right. Nearly twelve.'

'I could do with a drink. Hope they lay something on.'   10

'I'm sure they will. The Wilcoxes say they're awfully nice people. Not really the schoolmaster-type at all, Sally says.'

The man said, 'He's an Oxford chap.'

'Is he? You didn't say.'

'Mmn.'   15

'Of course, the fees are that much higher than the Seaford place.'

'Fifty quid or so. We'll have to see.'

The car turned right, between white gates and high, dark, tight-clipped hedges. The whisper of the road under the tyres changed to the crunch of gravel. The child, staring sideways, read black lettering on a white board: 'St Edward's Preparatory School. Please Drive Slowly'. He shifted on the seat, and the leather sucked at the bare skin under his knees, stinging.

The mother said, 'It's a lovely place. Those must be the playing-fields. Look, darling, there are some of the boys.' She clicked open her handbag, and the sun caught her mirror and flashed in the child's eyes; the comb went through her hair and he saw the grooves it left, neat as distant ploughing.

'Come on, then, Charles, out you get.'

The building was red brick, early nineteenth century, spreading out long arms in which windows glittered blackly. Flowers, trapped in neat beds, were alternate red and white. They went up the steps, the man, the woman, and the child two paces behind.

The woman, the mother, smoothing down a skirt that would be ridged from sitting, thought: I like the way they've got the maid all done up properly. The little white apron and all that. She's foreign, I suppose. Au pair. Very nice. If he comes here there'll be Speech Days and that kind of thing. Sally Wilcox says it's quite dressy – she got that cream linen coat for coming down here. You can see why it costs a bomb. Great big grounds and only an hour and a half from London.

They went into a room looking out into a terrace. Beyond, dappled lawns, gently shifting trees, black and white cows grazing behind iron railings. Books, leather chairs, a table with magazines – *Country Life*, *The Field*, *The Economist*. 'Please, if you would wait here. The Headmaster won't be long.'

Alone, they sat, inspected. 'I like the atmosphere, don't you, John?'

'Very pleasant, yes.' Four hundred a term, near enough. You can tell it's a cut above the Seaford place, though, or the one at St Albans. Bob Wilcox says quite a few City people send their boys here. One or two of the merchant bankers, those kind of people. It's the sort of contact that would do no harm at all. You meet someone, get talking at a cricket match or what have you... Not at all a bad thing.

'All right, Charles? You didn't get sick in the car, did you?'

The child had black hair, slicked down smooth to his head. His ears, too large, jutted out, transparent in the light from the window, laced with tiny, delicate veins. His clothes had the shine and crease of newness. He looked at the books, the dark brown pictures, his parents, said nothing.

20

25

30

35

40

45

50

'Come here, let me tidy your hair.'

The door opened. The child hesitated, stood up, sat, then rose again with his father.

'Mr and Mrs Manders? How very nice to meet you – I'm Margaret Spokes, and will you please forgive my husband who is tied up with some wretch who broke the cricket pavilion window and will be just a few more minutes. We try to be organised but a schoolmaster's day is always just that bit unpredictable. Do please sit down and what will you have to revive you after that beastly drive? You live in Finchley, is that right?'

55

60

'Hampstead, really,' said the mother. 'Sherry would be lovely.' She worked over the headmaster's wife from shoes to hairstyle, pricing and assessing. Shoes old but expensive – Russell and Bromley. Good skirt. Blouse could be Marks and Sparks – not sure. Real pearls. Super Victorian ring. She's not gone to any particular trouble – that's just what she'd wear anyway. You can be confident, with a voice like that, of course. Sally Wilcox says she knows all sorts of people.

65

The headmaster's wife said, 'I don't know how much you know about us? Prospectuses don't tell you a thing do they. We'll look round everything in a minute, when you've had a chat with my husband. I gather you're friends of the Wilcoxes, by the way. I'm awfully fond of Simon – he's down for Winchester, of course, but I expect you know that.'

70

The mother smiled over her sherry. Oh, I know that all right. Sally Wilcox doesn't let you forget that.

'And this is Charles? My dear, we've been forgetting all about you! In a minute I'm going to borrow Charles and take him off to meet some of the boys because after all you're choosing a school for him, aren't you, and not for you, so he ought to know what he might be letting himself in for and it shows we've got nothing to hide.'

75

The parents laughed. The father, sherry warming his guts, thought that this was an amusing woman. Not attractive, of course, a bit homespun, but impressive all the same. Partly the voice, of course; it takes a bloody expensive education to produce a voice like that. And other things, of course. Background and all that stuff.

'I think I can hear the thud of the Fourth Form coming in from games, which means my husband is on his way, and then I shall leave you with him while I take Charles off to the common room.'

For a moment the three adults centred on the child, looking, judging. The mother said, 'He looks so hideously pale, compared to those boys we saw outside.'

'My dear, that's London, isn't it? You just have to get them out, to get some colour into them. Ah, here's James. James – Mr and Mrs Manders. You remember, Bob Wilcox was mentioning at Sports Day...'

The headmaster reflected his wife's style, like paired cards in Happy Families. His clothes were mature rather than old, his skin well-scrubbed, his shoes clean, his geniality untainted by the least condescension. He was genuinely sorry to have kept them waiting, but in this business one lurches from one minor crisis to the next... And this is Charles? Hello, there, Charles. His large hand rested for a moment on the child's head, quite extinguishing the thin, dark hair. It was as though he had but to clench his fingers to crush the skull. But he took his hand away and moved the parents to the window, to observe the mutilated cricket pavilion, with indulgent laughter.

And the child is borne away by the headmaster's wife. She never touches him or tells him to come, but simply bears him away like some relentless tide, down corridors and through swinging glass doors, towing him like a frail craft, not bothering to look back to see if he is following, confident in the strength of magnetism, or obedience.

And delivers him to a room where boys are scattered among inky tables and rungless chairs and sprawled on a mangy carpet. There is a scampering, and a rising, and a silence falling, as she opens the door.

'Now this is the Lower Third, Charles, who you'd be with if you come to us in September. Boys, this is Charles Manders, and I want you to tell him all about things and answer any questions he wants to ask. You can believe about half of what they say, Charles, and they will tell you the most fearful lies about the food, which is excellent.'

The boys laugh and groan; amiable, exaggerated groans. They must like the headmaster's wife: there is licensed repartee. They look at her with bright eyes in open, eager faces. Someone leaps to hold the door for her, and close it behind her. She is gone.

The child stands in the centre of the room, and it draws in around him. The circle of children contracts, faces are only a yard or so from him, strange faces, looking, assessing.

Asking questions. They help themselves to his name, his age, his school. Over their heads he sees beyond the window an inaccessible world of shivering trees and high racing clouds and his voice which has floated like a feather in the dusty schoolroom air dies altogether and he becomes mute, and he stands in the middle of them with shoulders humped, staring down at feet: grubby plimsolls and kicked brown sandals. There is a noise in his ears like rushing water, a torrential din out of which voices boom, blotting each other out so that he cannot always hear the words. Do you? they say, and Have you? and What's your? and the faces, if he looks up, swing into one another in kaleidoscopic patterns and the floor under his feet is unsteady, lifting and falling. 120

125

And out of the noises comes one voice that is complete, that he can hear. 'Next term we'll mash you,' it says. 'We always mash new boys.' 130

And a bell goes, somewhere beyond doors and down corridors, and suddenly the children are all gone, clattering away and leaving him there with the heaving floor and the walls that shift and swing, and the headmaster's wife comes back and tows him away, and he is with his parents again, and they are getting into the car, and the high hedges skim past the car windows once more, in the other direction, and the gravel under the tyres changes to black tarmac. 135

'Well?'

'I liked it, didn't you?' The mother adjusted the car around her, closing windows, shrugging into her seat. 140

'Very pleasant, really. Nice chap.'

'I like him. Not quite so sure about her.'

'It's pricey, of course.'

'All the same…'

'Money well spent, though. One way and another.' 145

'Shall we settle it, then?'

'I think so. I'll drop him a line.'

The mother pitched her voice a notch higher to speak to the child in the back of the car. 'Would you like to go there, Charles? Like Simon Wilcox. Did you see that lovely gym, and the swimming-pool? And did the other boys tell you all about it?' 150

The child does not answer. He looks straight ahead of him, at the road coiling beneath the bonnet of the car. His face is haggard with anticipation.

8 How writers describe people

▶ Which of the details in the following extract do you think tell you most about the boy? Discuss this in your group, and then work out how you are going to justify your choice to the other groups.

> The child had black hair, slicked down smooth to his head. His ears, too large, jutted out, transparent in the light from the window, laced with tiny, delicate veins. His clothes had the shine and crease of newness. He looked at the books, the dark brown pictures, his parents, said nothing.
>
> 'Come here, let me tidy your hair.'
>
> The door opened. The child hesitated, stood up, sat, then rose again with his father.

9 Describing your chosen people

▶ Write one paragraph about one of the people you meet on arrival at the place you have chosen for your story.
▶ You might like to include details about:
  a external features of the person, such as height, clothes and hair style.
  b body language, such as the way they react to your arrival.
  c anything that will help the reader understand their character, e.g. by what they say or do.

10 How writers describe places

▶ Which of the details in the following extracts do you think tell you most about the kind of school Charles is going to? Discuss in your group, and then work out how you are going to justify your choice to the other groups.

> The car turned right, between white gates and high, dark, tight-clipped hedges. The whisper of the road under the tyres changed to the crunch of gravel. The child, staring sideways, read black lettering on a white board: 'St Edward's Preparatory School. Please Drive Slowly'.

> The building was red brick, early nineteenth century, spreading out long arms in which windows glittered blackly. Flowers, trapped in neat beds, were alternate red and white.

> They went into a room looking out into a terrace. Beyond, dappled lawns, gently shifting trees, black and white cows grazing behind iron railings. Books, leather chairs, a table with magazines – *Country Life*, *The Field*, *The Economist*.

ADVICE

▲ Don't choose a whole paragraph as that is too vague. Select a precise detail that you find effective and work out why it is effective.

11 Describing your chosen place

▶ Write one paragraph describing the place you have chosen for your story.

▶ You might like to include details about:

    a first impressions from the outside, e.g. the size of the building and if it is welcoming, threatening, etc.

    b first impressions from the inside, e.g. the height and size of rooms, any particular things you notice (select the most effective of the five senses here).

12 Exploring feelings

▶ Which of the following details tell you most about the way Charles is feeling? Be ready to justify your decision to the other groups.

> The child stands in the centre of the room, and it draws in around him. The circle of children contracts, faces are only a yard or so from him, strange faces, looking, assessing.
>
> Asking questions. They help themselves to his name, his age, his school. Over their heads he sees beyond the window an inaccessible world of shivering trees and high racing clouds and his voice which has floated like a feather in the dusty schoolroom air dies altogether and he becomes mute, and he stands in the middle of them with shoulders humped, staring down at feet: grubby plimsolls and kicked brown sandals. There is a noise in his ears like rushing water, a torrential din out of which voices boom, blotting each other out so that he cannot always hear the words. Do you? they say, and Have you? and What's your? and the faces, if he looks up, swing into one another in kaleidoscopic patterns and the floor under his feet is unsteady, lifting and falling.

13 Exploring endings and the story as a whole

▶ Re-read the last few lines of the story.

> 'Shall we settle it, then?'
>
> 'I think so. I'll drop him a line.'
>
> The mother pitched her voice a notch higher to speak to the child in the back of the car. 'Would you like to go there, Charles? Like Simon Wilcox. Did you see that lovely gym, and the swimming-pool? And did the other boys tell you all about it?'
>
> The child does not answer. He looks straight ahead of him, at the road coiling beneath the bonnet of the car. His face is haggard with anticipation.

▶ Discuss the following questions in your group:

    a What have the parents decided to 'settle'?

    b Why does the mother ask Charles the questions?

    c Why doesn't Charles answer?

    d What can you tell about Charles's thoughts and feelings?

    e Do you find the ending interesting/effective/confusing/annoying? Why?

    f Taking the story as a whole, which is the most important crisis or turning point?

    g Taking the story as a whole, whose side is the author on, if any? (The boy's? The headmaster's wife's? The parents'?) How can you tell?

The story

14 Writing a story

▶ Write a story about arriving at a new place for the first time.

▶ You may find you can use many of the shorter pieces you have written in preparation, but make sure the joins aren't obvious.

▶ The most important aim is to learn from the techniques you have identified in other writers' work.

▶ Here is a checklist to remind you as you write:

a Have you made the opening special to this particular event and day, perhaps withholding some information to create suspense?

b Have you described the place convincingly, giving readers who have never been there a strong picture in their mind?

c Have you described any people involved convincingly, so the reader believes they do exist?

d Have you included details about how any problems/anxieties develop, leading to a clear turning point or moment of crisis?

e Have you described your own thoughts and feelings so that a reader understands as fully as possible how you reacted to this first visit?

f Have you started a new paragraph where appropriate, e.g. for a shift in time or place?

g Have you ended your story in an interesting (and satisfying) way?

Self-assessment

15 Judging your own performance

▶ From the list below:
  a select three points on which you feel you have made the most progress.
  b select one point on which you most need to improve.
  I can explain what details make an opening effective.
  I can explain what details make a description effective.
  I can explain what details make a character convincing.
  I can explain what details make an ending effective.
  I can write a story with an opening that fits that story effectively.
  I can write a description of a place which allows a reader to imagine it clearly.
  I can write about people so that the reader is convinced they are real (even if I have invented them).
  I can write an effective ending to a story.

16 Improving your skills in English

▶ Select one or two skills you need to concentrate on to improve your skills in writing. (The descriptions of levels are a guide, not a rulebook.)

	Writing skill	From	To
1	Vocabulary choices are adventurous and words are used for effect	Level 3	Level 4
2	Writing is lively and thoughtful, and is sustained and developed in an interesting way	Level 3	Level 4
3	Vocabulary choices are imaginative and words are used precisely	Level 4	Level 5
4	Writing is varied and interesting	Level 4	Level 5
5	Use a range of sentence structures and varied vocabulary to create effects	Level 5	Level 6
6	Writing engages and sustains the reader's interest	Level 5	Level 6
7	Grammatical features and vocabulary are accurately and effectively used	Level 6	Level 7
8	Characters and settings are developed	Level 6	Level 7
9	The use of vocabulary and grammar enables fine distinctions to be made	Level 7	Above Level 7
10	Control of characters, events and settings	Level 7	Above Level 7

10 Exploring Shakespeare Global

Your focus

The content of this unit is designed to:
● explore the way Shakespeare wrote for the theatre
● help you understand more about Shakespeare's plays
● help you appreciate a playwright's choices.

Your target

By the end of this unit you should be more able to:
● understand why language changes over time
● understand the choices authors make in writing for the theatre
● appreciate how a text comes to life in a live theatre production.

Your move

Reading

Speaking and listening

16 Improving your skills in English

15 Judging your own performance

Self-assessment

10 Brutus and the assassination of Caesar

Brutus and Mark Antony

Shakespeare's Julius Caesar

Exploring Shakespeare

1 Reading a picture

The wheel of fortune

2 Exploring how language changes over time

Two views of Julius Caesar

3 Comparing two versions

4 Heroes or villains?

Shakespeare's Globe Theatre

11 Illustrating an image

7 Exploring the storyline of Shakespeare's Julius Caesar

6 Being a spectator in Shakespeare's theatre

5 Finding out about the Globe

12 Heroes or villains?

14 Exploring the reasons for including the two speeches

8 Exploring Shakespeare's technique

9 Can we predict or change the future?

13 Investigating rhetoric

The wheel of fortune

1 Reading a picture

▶ In pairs, note down what you think are the five most important things included in the picture of the wheel of fortune.

▶ Create a storyline to explain what is happening in the picture. You should try to make sense of as much of the picture as possible.

▶ Share your ideas in a group of four and decide on the best combined storyline, preparing to explain to the other groups how your storyline makes sense of details from the picture.

▶ In your groups of two, write a caption for the picture in not more than 15 words. The caption should sum up the 'central message' of the picture.

Two views of Julius Caesar

In this unit you will be looking at different versions of the assassination of Julius Caesar.

The first extract (on the left) is by Geoffrey Chaucer, who did most of his writing between about 1368 and 1400. It is taken from The Monk's Tale (part of the *Canterbury Tales*). The Monk (who mistakenly treats Brutus and Cassius as one person) is trying to prove that anyone who is successful and powerful is bound to end up unsuccessful and powerless sooner or later.

The second extract (on the right) is a version of the same lines as the first, but was written in 1964.

De Julio Cesare

By wisedom, manhede, and by greet labour,
From humble bed to roial magestee
Up roos he Julius, the conquerour,
That wan al th'occident by land and see,
By strengthe of hand, or elles by tretee,   5
And unto Rome make hem tributarie;
And sitthe of Rome the emperour was he
Til that Fortune weex his adversarie.

To Rome agayn repaireth Julius
With his triumphe, lauriat ful hye;   10
But on a tyme Brutus Cassius,
That evere hadde of his hye estaat envye,
Ful prively hath maad conspiracye
Agayns this Julius in subtil wise,
And caste the place in which he sholde dye   15
With boydekyns, as I shal yow devyse.

This Julius to the Capitolie wente
Upon a day, as he was wont to goon,
And in the Capitolie anon hym hente
This false Brutus, and his othere foon,   20
And stiked hym with boydekyns anoon
With many a wounde, and thus they lete hym lye;
But nevere gronte he at no strook but oon,
Or elles at two, but if his storie lye.

Of Julius Caesar

Through wisdom, valour, and immense labour the conqueror Julius raised himself from a humble station to royal majesty, gaining the whole Occident, land and sea, by diplomacy or force of arms, and making it tributary to Rome, of which he later became Emperor: till Fortune turned against him.

Julius returned again to his triumph in Rome, crowned with laurels; but in time Brutus Cassius, who had always envied his great eminence, secretly wove a subtle conspiracy against Julius and (as I shall relate) chose the spot where he was to be killed with daggers.

Julius went to the Capitol as usual one day, and there he was suddenly set upon by the treacherous Brutus and other of his enemies who stabbed him with their daggers and left him lying covered with wounds. Yet he groaned only at one of these blows, or at the most two, unless history is mistaken.

2 Exploring how language changes over time

▶ Match up words from the Chaucer version with the words used in the 1964 version.

Fourteenth-century Middle English	Twentieth-century modern English
wisedom (line 1)	
roial (line 2)	
magestee (line 2)	
see (line 4)	
Fortune (line 8)	
triumphe (line 10)	
hadde of his hye estaat envye (line 12)	
conspiracye (line 13)	
stiked (line 21)	
boydekyns (line 21)	

▶ Are you surprised at how much the language has changed or how little the language has changed over this time period?
▶ What words do your parents and grandparents use that you would choose not to use? Why?
▶ Do you pronounce some words differently from the way your parents and grandparents pronounce them? Why?
▶ What words do you use that your parents and grandparents do not use? Why?
▶ Why do you think language changes over time?

3 Comparing two versions

▶ Can you find any pattern to the rhyming in the Chaucer original?
▶ The Chaucer original is in verse, but the 1964 version is in prose. Why do you think the modern author chose to write his version in prose?

ADVICE

▲ Think back to when you were writing your own riddles in Unit 5. What did you find if you tried to rhyme many of the lines?
▲ 'hye' in line 10 of the Chaucer version does mean 'high'. What did Chaucer rhyme this with? What's the problem and why?

4 Heroes or villains?

▶ Is Julius Caesar presented as a hero or a villain? Select four short quotations from the 1964 version which help you decide, and make a note of them in your own table.
▶ Is Brutus Cassius presented as a hero or a villain? Select four short quotations from the 1964 version which help you decide, and make a note of them.
▶ Use only a few words – a maximum of four – in each case.

Julius Caesar	Hero or villain?	Brutus Cassius	Hero or villain?

Shakespeare's Globe Theatre

5 Finding out about the Globe

▶ The following two texts are extracts from the Internet.

▶ Read through both texts, thinking about what it would have been like to be part of the audience in this kind of theatre in Shakespeare's day.

Home   Site Info   Old Globe   New Globe   Research

The Shakespeare Globe Exhibition

New Globe Walk
Bankside
London
SE1 9DT
Tel: +44 (0)20 7902 1500
Fax: +44 (0)20 7902 1515
Web: www.shakespeares-globe.org

The first Globe was built in Southwark in 1599. The Globe was at the heart of Shakespeare's London, the Elizabethan equivalent of Shaftesbury Avenue or Broadway and the main theatrical entertainment district of London. Unfortunately, the theatre was burnt down in 1613 when a prop cannon shot an ember into the thatched roof during a performance of Henry VIII.

Now, nearly 400 years later, Shakespeare's Globe is a reconstruction of the original Southwark theatre. The Shakespeare Globe Centre is an educational, cultural and entertainment centre which includes a museum under the theatre, research facilities and an exhibition of Elizabethan London.

Shakespeare's Globe Trust is dedicated to the experience and international understanding of Shakespeare in performance. Uniquely its work celebrates the fact that the greatest dramatic poet in the English language lived and worked in London and that the cradle of English theatre was on Bankside by the River Thames.

In 1996, Shakespeare's Globe was voted the best attraction in Europe and it was awarded the European Tourism Initiative Golden Star Award by the European Federation of Associations of Tourism Journalists.

Groups must book in advance.

For further information please visit the Globe Website.

English Department   The University of Reading

This page originated by Chantal Miller-Schütz
Revised by Lyn Holman

Last modified on 20th March, 2000

Home   Site Info   Old Globe   New Globe   Research

The reconstructed Globe stage

The Globe Theatre presents a lavishly painted stage in the heart of the 'Wooden 'O' '.

- On the balcony you might see musicians or members of the audience (in Shakespeare's day, the richer patrons, now mostly guests of the company).
- Left and right of the stage, on the middle gallery, are the Gentlemen's Rooms, the Renaissance equivalent of corporate boxes, which also provide the most comfortable seating.
- The pillars hold up the Heavens and provide hiding-places for the actors.
- The three galleries offer benches and mostly good sightlines.
- In the yard, for £5, the modern equivalent of the penny paid by Shakespeare's groundlings, you can stand and have the closest view of the actors that you will ever get in any theatre.

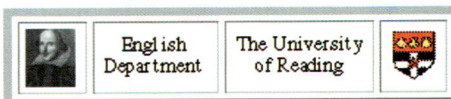

| | English Department | The University of Reading | |

This page originated by Chantal Miller-Schütz
Revised by Lyn Holman

Last modified on 10th February, 2000

- Shakespeare wrote his first plays well before the opening of the Globe Theatre. Between what years could you have seen a Shakespeare play in the original Globe Theatre?
- Give one example of a prop used in the theatre during that time.
- How does the first extract describe Shakespeare?
- Why do you think a new theatre, matching the design of the old theatre, has been built?

WORDS

▲ **box** *noun* in a theatre, etc: a separate compartment for a group of people containing several seats.
▲ **corporate** *adjective* relating to companies or the people, especially the executives, who work in them.
▲ **groundling** *noun* a spectator who stood in the pit of an Elizabethan theatre.
▲ **patron** *noun* someone who gives financial support and encouragement e.g. to an artist, the arts, a movement or charity.
▲ **prop** *noun* (short for *property*) any article or object used in a play or film other than painted scenery or costumes.

6 Being a spectator in Shakespeare's theatre

▶ The audience can view the play from the balcony, the Gentlemen's Rooms, the three galleries and the yard.

▶ Decide which you think would have been best for:

a comfort.   b price.

c involvement in the play.   d overall view of the stage.

▶ 1 = best; 4 = worst.

▶ Remember that the three galleries would be to the left, right and behind you if you were standing where the picture of the stage on page 120 was taken.

▶ Use tables like the ones below to record your decisions.

Comfort

Seating area	Rating 1–4	Explanation
Balcony		
Gentlemen's Rooms		
Three galleries		
Yard		

Price

Seating area	Rating 1–4	Explanation
Balcony		
Gentlemen's Rooms		
Three galleries		
Yard		

Involvement in the play

Seating area	Rating 1–4	Explanation
Balcony		
Gentlemen's Rooms		
Three galleries		
Yard		

Overall view of the stage

Seating area	Rating 1–4	Explanation
Balcony		
Gentlemen's Rooms		
Three galleries		
Yard		

Shakespeare's Julius Caesar

7 Exploring the storyline of Shakespeare's Julius Caesar

▶ One of Shakespeare's plays is based on the life of Julius Caesar.

▶ Discuss and decide in pairs the storyline of the play by looking at the following graphic novel version, which covers the first half of the play.

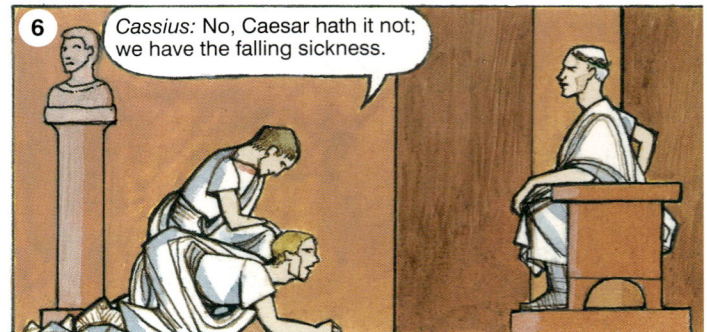

1 *Soothsayer:* Beware the ides of March.

2 *Caesar:* He is a dreamer; let us leave him.

3 *Crowd:* Caesar!

4 *Cassius:* The fault, dear Brutus, is not in our stars, But in ourselves, that we are underlings. Why should that name be sounded more than yours?

5 *Brutus:* He hath the falling sickness.

Casca: He fell down in the market-place.

6 *Cassius:* No, Caesar hath it not; we have the falling sickness.

7 *Brutus:* Crown him – that! And then, I grant, we put a sting in him.

8 *Brutus:* Think him as a serpent's egg. And kill him in the shell.

9 Cassius: Let us swear our resolution.

10 Brutus: Let's kill him boldly, but not wrathfully.

11 Portia: You have some sick offence within your mind, which by the right and virtue of my place I ought to know of.

12 Calphurnia: What mean you, Caesar? Think you to walk forth? You shall not stir out of your house today.

13 Caesar: The ides of March are come.

14 Soothsayer: Ay, Caesar, but not gone.

15

Later, Caesar is stabbed by Cassius and Brutus.

16 Caesar: Et tu, Brute? – Then fall, Caesar!

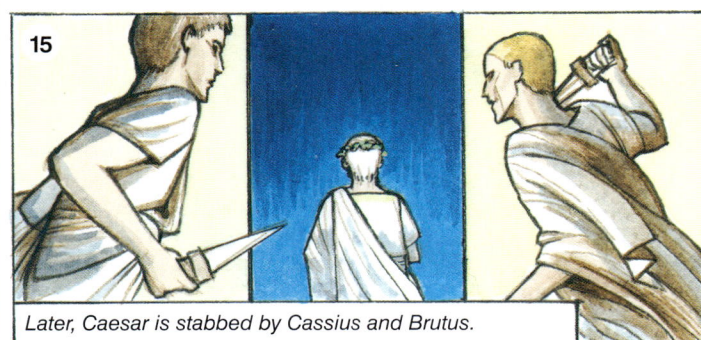

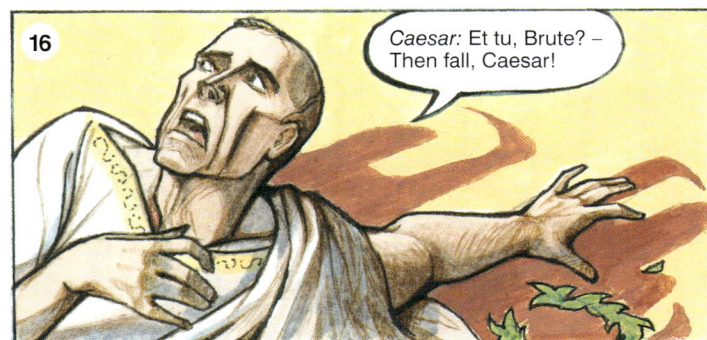

▶ Calphurnia, wife of Julius Caesar, and Portia, wife of Brutus, are the only female characters in the play. In your group, brainstorm the possible reasons for this. Then select the reason you are most confident about for reporting back to the other groups.

▶ In pairs, prepare to tell your version of the storyline illustrated above to the other groups.

WORDS

▲ **ides** *noun* in the ancient Roman calendar: the fifteenth day of March, May, July and October, and the thirteenth day of the other months.

▲ **soothsayer** *noun* someone who predicts the future.

▲ **underling** *noun* a subordinate or inferior.

8 Exploring Shakespeare's technique

▶ Match each of the frames listed below with the technique Shakespeare could be using. Eight techniques (**A** to **H**) are provided.

▶ Some of the techniques could match more than one frame. You decide which ones fit best where, overall.

Frame	Technique(s)
1	
3	
5	
7	
8	
9	
14	
15	

ADVICE

▲ You will need to refer to the full version on pages 122 and 123.
▲ Match up the ones you find easiest first, then the choices will become easier.

Techniques

A Short, sharp reply – might send a shiver down the spine.

B Use of dramatic action – might increase the heart rate of those in the audience.

C Use of senses – sight: darkness to create atmosphere of something secret and dangerous.

D Use of senses – sound: loud sound to engage the audience's attention.

E Use of a simile/an image.

F Use of a soliloquy – one character's private thoughts spoken aloud.

G Use of suspense – makes the audience wonder what will happen later in the play.

H Uses characters on stage to describe events that have happened off-stage.

9 Can we predict or change the future?

▶ One theme running through the play is how far we control our own lives.

▶ Think back to the picture of the wheel of fortune on page 116 and Chaucer's version of the assassination of Julius Caesar on page 117. Remember that the monk is arguing that everyone who has a high position in life will sooner or later lose their power and influence. Chaucer's monk suggests that Julius Caesar could not change his future even if he was warned about it.

▶ Discuss the following questions in your group and decide which answers you come up with are best. (Don't expect easy answers!)

a Do you think Shakespeare's soothsayer suggests that Julius Caesar could avoid being assassinated? How can you tell?

b What does Cassius have to say about believing in the stars as an influence on our lives?

c Prepare to read your own twenty-first-century language version of what Cassius says in Frame 4 to the other groups.

WORDS

▲ **fate** *noun* the apparent power that determines the course of events, over which humans have no control.

▲ **fortune** *noun* 1 chance as a force in human affairs; fate. 2 luck.

▲ **the stars** *noun* the planets regarded as an influence on people's fortunes.

▲ **wheel of fortune** *noun* the wheel believed to be spun by Fortune, the symbol of change, consequently bringing about changes in people's lives.

Brutus and Mark Antony

10 Brutus and the assassination of Caesar

▶ Read the speech below by Brutus from Shakespeare's play, which he wrote in about 1600. Brutus is on his own in his orchard in Rome (as in Frame 7 on page 122). He is thinking aloud about Caesar and whether Caesar should be assassinated. This type of speech, where the audience hears the private thoughts of a character on stage, is called a soliloquy.

It must be by his death; and for my part,
I know no personal cause to spurn at him,
But for the general: he would be crown'd.
How that might change his nature, there's the question.
It is the bright day that brings forth the adder, 5
And that craves wary walking. Crown him – that!
And then, I grant, we put a sting in him
That at his will he may do danger with.
Th'abuse of greatness is, when it disjoins
Remorse from power; and to speak truth of Caesar, 10
I have not known when his affections sway'd
More than his reason. But 'tis a common proof
That lowliness is young ambition's ladder,
Whereto the climber-upward turns his face;
But when he once attains the upmost round, 15
He then unto the ladder turns his back,
Looks in the clouds, scorning the base degrees
By which he did ascend. So Caesar may.
Then, lest he may, prevent. And since the quarrel
Will bear no colour for the thing he is, 20
Fashion it thus – that what he is, augmented,
Would run to these and these extremities;
And therefore think him as a serpent's egg,
Which, hatch'd, would as his kind grow mischievous,
And kill him in the shell. 25

WORDS

▲ **disjoins** *verb* separates ('dis-' is a prefix meaning 'do the opposite of').
▲ **mischievous** *adjective* harmful.
▲ **remorse** *noun* compassion; pity.
▲ **upmost** *adjective* uppermost.

Summaries

A Caesar is not actually an evil man now, but if he was crowned, he might become a dangerous dictator.
B If he might turn out dangerous, it's better to deal with him now before he becomes dangerous.
C Most people, when they get power, forget what they were like before and look down on the friends they had before.
D Caesar wants to be crowned, and power changes people for the worse.
E The most dangerous people are those who have power but have no feelings for other human beings.

▶ Match up the following parts of Brutus's speech with the summaries **A** to **E** above.

Lines	Section of Brutus's speech	Match up with A to E above
3–5	he would be crown'd… brings forth the adder,	
6–8	Crown him – that!… do danger with.	
9–10	Th'abuse of greatness… Remorse from power;	
15–18	when he once attains… By which he did ascend.	
23–25	think him as a serpent's egg… kill him in the shell.	

▶ Does the word 'mischievous' mean the same thing today? Write a dictionary definition, using the pattern of a published dictionary entry, for what you think ' mischievous' means in the twenty-first century. Add an example of usage – a typical sentence someone might use that includes the word 'mischievous'.

11 Illustrating an image

▶ Choose one of the following images from Brutus's speech and design a cartoon, picture or diagram to illustrate what is suggested by the image. You can use a single illustration or a series of illustrations. The important thing is to get the point across in a *visual* way.

a 'The bright day that brings forth the adder' (dangerous snakes like adders are more likely to come out when the sun is out; Caesar is more likely to be dangerous when he is praised and crowned).

b 'Crown him – that!/And then, I grant, we put a sting in him/That at his will he may do danger with' (if we crown him, we give him the power (sting) to do too much of what he wants when he wants).

c 'Lowliness is young ambition's ladder,/Whereto the climber-upward turns his face;/But when he once attains the upmost round,/He then unto the ladder turns his back,/Looks in the clouds, scorning the base degrees/By which he did ascend' (if someone is ambitious, they will use other people to get on in life; but once they get to the top of the 'ladder' they will ignore those who helped them on their way).

d 'A serpent's egg,/Which, hatch'd, would as his kind grow mischievous,/And kill him in the shell' (it's as if Caesar is in a shell at the moment – if he is crowned and given power, it will be like opening the shell and seeing that what is inside is a dangerous serpent).

12 Heroes or villains?

▶ Later in the play, Brutus tries to explain to a crowd of citizens why he has helped to assassinate Julius Caesar.

▶ Read the following speeches, and decide if you support Brutus or Mark Antony.

BRUTUS

If there be any in this assembly, any dear friend of Caesar's, to him I say that Brutus' love to Caesar was no less than his. If then that friend demand why Brutus rose against Caesar, this is my answer: Not that I lov'd Caesar less, but that I lov'd Rome more. Had you rather Caesar were living, and die all slaves, than that Caesar were dead, to live all free men? As Caesar lov'd me, I weep for him; as he was fortunate, I rejoice at it; as he was valiant, I honour him; but – as he was ambitious, I slew him.

Brutus succeeds in persuading the crowd that he was right to help assassinate Caesar. He is so successful that some in the crowd suggest he should be crowned as the new Caesar. Mark Antony now tries to persuade the same crowd in a totally different way. He says that Caesar was not ambitious, as Brutus claims, but actually refused to be king.

MARK ANTONY
You all did see that on the Lupercal
I thrice presented him a kingly crown,
Which he did thrice refuse. Was this ambition?
Yet Brutus says he was ambitious;
And sure he is an honourable man.
I speak not to disprove what Brutus spoke,
But here I am to speak what I do know.
You all did love him once, not without cause;
What cause withholds you, then, to mourn for him?
O judgment, thou art fled to brutish beasts,
And men have lost their reason!

▶ In your groups, discuss these questions and prepare to report back to the other groups.

a Do you think Shakespeare is presenting Julius Caesar as a hero or a villain here? Use both speeches to explain your answer.

b Do you think Shakespeare is presenting Brutus as a hero or a villain here? Use both speeches to explain your answer.

13 Investigating rhetoric

▶ Look at the way Brutus's speech is laid out on page 126 compared with the way Mark Antony's speech is laid out. What is the difference? What is each type of text called?

▶ You now have the task of helping someone else perform Brutus's speech aloud. Some parts of the speech are balanced:

Not   that I lov'd   Caesar   less,
but   that I lov'd   Rome   more.

▶ Re-write the section of Brutus's speech below, using any methods you can think of to make patterns like these clear.

> Not that I lov'd Caesar less, but that I lov'd Rome more. Had you rather Caesar were living, and die all slaves, than that Caesar were dead, to live all free men? As Caesar lov'd me, I weep for him; as he was fortunate, I rejoice at it; as he was valiant, I honour him; but – as he was ambitious, I slew him.

▶ One person from your group should now act as an envoy, taking your version to another group. Ask them to read it to you, following your guidelines.

▶ When you return to your own group, tell the others what worked and what did not work. Make any necessary revisions. For example, the other group may have decided that the gaps you have left indicated long pauses, and they read it out with long gaps which sounded unconvincing.

▶ Now prepare to read your version to the other groups, making the patterns of language clear but not obvious.

WORDS

▲ **rhetoric** *noun* the art of speaking and writing well, especially in order to persuade or influence others.

ADVICE

You could use:
▲ the position of the text on the page.
▲ highlighter pens.
▲ arrows.
▲ underlining.
▲ any combination of these.
▲ your own ideas.
It may help to look for opposites (less/more), repeated patterns (that I lov'd/that I lov'd) and deliberate contrasts (Caesar/Rome).

14 Exploring the reasons for including the two speeches

▶ In the extracts above, Shakespeare has one character blaming Caesar and one character praising Caesar.

▶ Why do you think Shakespeare included both the speech by Brutus over Caesar's dead body, and the speech by Mark Antony? Rate each of the following statements according to how far you think they are likely reasons.

▶ Prepare to explain your decisions to the other groups. Your notes should show clearly why you came to each decision.

Statements	Very likely	Quite likely	Not at all likely
Shakespeare couldn't decide whose side he was on			
Shakespeare thought it would be more powerful in the theatre to sway the theatre audience in the same way the audience in 'Rome' (on stage) are swayed			
Shakespeare wanted the audience to support Brutus when Brutus was speaking and Mark Antony when Mark Antony was speaking			
Shakespeare was clearly against the assassination			
Shakespeare wanted to encourage people in the audience to come to their own conclusions			

Self-assessment

15 Judging your own performance

▶ From the list below:
  a select three points on which you feel you have made the most progress.
  b select one point on which you most need to improve.
  I understand some of the reasons why language changes over time.
  I know that a play is written to be performed rather than just read privately.
  I recognise some of the techniques a playwright uses to make a play come alive.
  I have used inference to work out some of the plot of *Julius Caesar*.
  I can recognise when an author uses patterns in their language.
  I can read/perform a part of a speech, making these patterns clear to the audience.
  I understand why a playwright might choose not to use obvious heroes and obvious villains in a play.

16 Improving your skills in English

▶ Select one or two skills you need to concentrate on to improve your skills in reading. Then do the same for your speaking and listening skills. (The descriptions of levels are a guide, not a rulebook.)

Reading skill		From	To
1	Begin to use inference and deduction	Level 3	Level 4
2	Refer to the text when explaining views	Level 3	Level 4
3	Select essential points	Level 4	Level 5
4	Use inference and deduction where appropriate	Level 4	Level 5
5	Identify different layers of meaning	Level 5	Level 6
6	Comment on the significance and effect of details of the text	Level 5	Level 6
7	Show understanding of the ways in which meaning and information are conveyed	Level 6	Level 7
8	Select and synthesise a range of information from a variety of sources	Level 6	Level 7
9	Evaluate how authors achieve their effects through their use of linguistic, structural and presentational devices	Level 7	Above Level 7
10	Select and analyse information and ideas and comment on how these are conveyed in different texts	Level 7	Above Level 7

Speaking and listening skill		From	To
1	Talk and listen confidently, exploring and communicating ideas	Level 3	Level 4
2	Make contributions that are responsive to others' ideas and views	Level 3	Level 4
3	Pay close attention to what others say, ask questions and develop ideas	Level 4	Level 5
4	Make contributions which take account of others' views	Level 4	Level 5
5	Take an active part in discussion, using a variety of vocabulary and expression	Level 5	Level 6
6	Show understanding of ideas and sensitivity to others	Level 5	Level 6
7	Use vocabulary precisely and organise their talk to communicate clearly	Level 6	Level 7
8	Make significant contributions, evaluating others' ideas and varying when and how they participate	Level 6	Level 7
9	Structure what they say clearly, using apt vocabulary and appropriate intonation and emphasis	Level 7	Above Level 7
10	Make a range of contributions which show they have listened perceptively and are sensitive to the development of discussion	Level 7	Above Level 7